T0373772

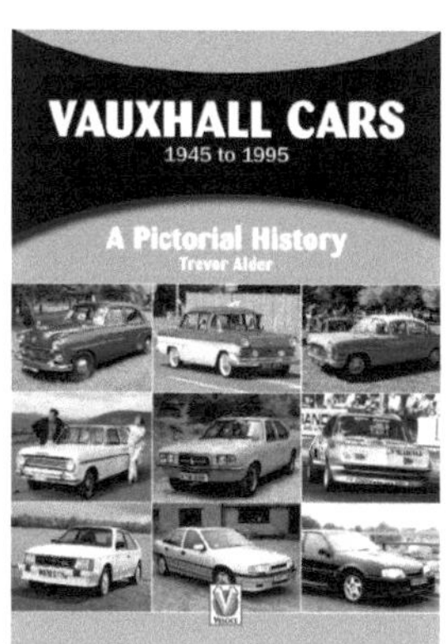
VAUXHALL CARS
1945 to 1995
A Pictorial History
Trevor Alder

VELOCE PUBLISHING
THE PUBLISHER OF FINE AUTOMOTIVE BOOKS

Enthusiast's Restoration Manual Series

Citroën 2CV Restore (Porter)
Classic British Car Electrical Systems (Astley)
Classic Car Bodywork, How to Restore (Thaddeus)
Classic Car Electrics (Thaddeus)
Classic Car Suspension, Steering & Wheels, How to Restore & Improve (Parish – translator)
Classic Cars, How to Paint (Thaddeus)
Classic Off-road Motorcycles, How to
Jaguar E-type (Crespin)
Reliant Regal, How to Restore (Payne)
Triumph TR2, 3, 3A, 4 & 4A, How to Restore (Williams)
Triumph TR5/250 & 6, How to Restore (Williams)
Triumph TR7/8, How to Restore (Williams)
Ultimate Mini Restoration Manual, The (Ayre & Webber)
Volkswagen Beetle, How to Restore (Tyler)
VW Bay Window Bus (Paxton)

A Pictorial History Series

Austin Cars 1948 to 1990 – A Pictorial History (Rowe)
Ford Cars (UK) – A Pictorial History (Rowe)
Morris Cars – 1948-1984 (Newell)
Rootes Cars of the 50s, 60s & 70s – Hillman, Humber, Singer, Sunbeam & Talbot, A Pictorial History (Rowe)
Rover Cars 1945 to 2005 – A Pictorial History (Taylor)
Triumph & Standard Cars 1945 to 1984 – A Pictorial History (Warrington)
Wolseley Cars 1948 to 1975 – A Pictorial History (Rowe)

Expert Guides

Land Rover Series I-III – Your expert guide to common problems & how to fix them (Thurman)
MG Midget & A-H Sprite – Your expert guide to common problems & how to fix them (Horler)
Triumph TR4 & TR4A – Your expert guide to common problems & how to fix them (Hogan)
Triumph TR6 – Your expert guide to common problems & how to fix them (Hogan)

Essential Buyer's Guide Series

Alfa Romeo Alfasud (Metcalfe)
Alfa Romeo Alfetta: all saloon/sedan models 1972 to 1984 & coupé models 1974 to 1987 (Metcalfe)
Alfa Romeo Giulia GT Coupé (Booker)
Alfa Romeo Giulia Spider (Booker)
Audi TT (Davies)
Audi TT Mk2 2006 to 2014 (Durnan)
Austin-Healey Big Healeys (Trummel)
BMW Boxer Twins (Henshaw)
BMW E30 3 Series 1981 to 1994 (Hosier)
BMW GS (Henshaw)
BMW X5 (Saunders)
BMW Z3 Roadster (Fishwick)
BMW Z4: E85 Roadster and E86 Coupé includingm and Alpina 2003 to 2009 (Smitheram)
BSA 350, 441 & 500 Singles (Henshaw)
BSA 500 & 650 Twins (Henshaw)
BSA Bantam (Henshaw)
Choosing, Using & Maintaining Your Electric Bicycle (Henshaw)
Citroën 2CV (Paxton)
Citroën DS & ID (Heilig)
Cobra Replicas (Ayre)
Corvette C2 Sting Ray 1963-1967 (Falconer)
Datsun 240Z 1969 to 1973 (Newlyn)
DeLorean DMC-12 1981 to 1983 (Williams)
Ducati Bevel Twins (Falloon)
Ducati Desmodue Twins (Falloon)
Ducati Desmoquattro Twins – 851, 888, 916, 996, 998, ST4 1988 to 2004 (Falloon)
Fiat 500 & 600 (Bobbitt)
Ford Capri (Paxton)
Ford Escort Mk1 & Mk2 (Williamson)
Ford Focus RS/ST 1st Generation (Williamson)
Ford Model A – All Models 1927 to 1931 (Buckley)
Ford Model T – All models 1909 to 1927 (Barker)
Ford Mustang – First Generation 1964 to 1973 (Cook)
Ford Mustang – Fifth Generation (2005-2014) (Cook)
Ford RS Cosworth Sierra & Escort (Williamson)
Harley-Davidson Big Twins (Henshaw)
Hillman Imp (Morgan)
Hinckley Triumph triples & fours 750, 900, 955, 1000, 1050, 1200 – 1991-2009 (Henshaw)
Honda CBR FireBlade (Henshaw)
Honda CBR600 Hurricane (Henshaw)
Honda SOHC Fours 1969-1984 (Henshaw)
Jaguar E-Type 3.8 & 4.2 litre (Crespin)
Jaguar E-type V12 5.3 litre (Crespin)
Jaguar Mark 1 & 2 (All models including Daimler 2.5-litre V8) 1955 to 1969 (Thorley)
Jaguar New XK 2005-2014 (Thorley)
Jaguar S-Type – 1999 to 2007 (Thorley)
Jaguar X-Type – 2001 to 2009 (Thorley)
Jaguar XJ-S (Crespin)
Jaguar XJ6, XJ8 & XJR (Thorley)
Jaguar XK 120, 140 & 150 (Thorley)
Jaguar XK8 & XKR (1996-2005) (Thorley)
Jaguar/Daimler XJ 1994-2003 (Crespin)
Jaguar/Daimler XJ40 (Crespin)
Jaguar/Daimler XJ6, XJ12 & Sovereign (Crespin)
Kawasaki Z1 & Z900 (Orritt)
Land Rover Discovery Series 1 (1989-1998) (Taylor)
Land Rover Discovery Series 2 (1998-2004) (Taylor)
Land Rover Series I, II & IIA (Thurman)
Land Rover Series III (Thurman)
Lotus Elan, S1 to Sprint and Plus 2 to Plus 2S 130/5 1962 to 1974 (Vale)
Lotus Europa, S1, S2, Twin-cam & Special 1966 to 1975 (Vale)
Lotus Seven replicas & Caterham 7: 1973-2013 (Hawkins)
Mazda MX-5 Miata (Mk1 1989-97 & Mk2 98-2001) (Crook)
Mazda RX-8 (Parish)
Mercedes-Benz 190: all 190 models (W201 series) 1982 to 1993 (Parish)
Mercedes-Benz 280-560SL & SLC (Bass)
Mercedes-Benz G-Wagen (Greene)
Mercedes-Benz Pagoda 230SL, 250SL & 280SL roadsters & coupés (Bass)
Mercedes-Benz S-Class W126 Series (Zoporowski)
Mercedes-Benz S-Class Second Generation W116 Series (Parish)
Mercedes-Benz SL R129-series 1989 to 2001 (Parish)
Mercedes-Benz SLK (Bass)
Mercedes-Benz W123 (Parish)
Mercedes-Benz W124 – All models 1984-1997 (Zoporowski)
MG Midget & A-H Sprite (Horler)
MG TD, TF & TF1500 (Jones)
MGA 1955-1962 (Crosier)
MGB & MGB GT (Williams)
MGF & MG TF (Hawkins)
Mini (Paxton)
Morgan Plus 4 (Benfield)
Morris Minor & 1000 (Newell)
Moto Guzzi 2-valve big twins (Falloon)
New Mini (Collins)
Norton Commando (Henshaw)
Peugeot 205 GTI (Blackburn)
Piaggio Scooters – all modern two-stroke & four-stroke automatic models 1991 to 2016 (Willis)
Porsche 356 (Johnson)
Porsche 911 (964) (Streather)
Porsche 911 (991) (Streather)
Porsche 911 (993) (Streather)
Porsche 911 (996) (Streather)
Porsche 911 (997) – Model years 2004 to 2009 (Streather)
Porsche 911 (997) – Second generation models 2009 to 2012 (Streather)
Porsche 911 Carrera 3.2 (Streather)
Porsche 911SC (Streather)
Porsche 924 – All models 1976 to 1988 (Hodgkins)
Porsche 928 (Hemmings)
Porsche 930 Turbo & 911 (930) Turbo (Streather)
Porsche 944 (Higgins)
Porsche 981 Boxster & Cayman (Streather)
Porsche 986 Boxster (Streather)
Porsche 987 Boxster and Cayman 1st generation (2005-2009) (Streather)
Porsche 987 Boxster and Cayman 2nd generation (2009-2012) (Streather)
Range Rover – First Generation models 1970 to 1996 (Taylor)
Range Rover – Second Generation 1994-2001 (Taylor)
Range Rover – Third Generation L322 (2002-2012) (Taylor)
Reliant Scimitar GTE (Payne)
Rolls-Royce Silver Shadow & Bentley T-Series (Bobbitt)
Rover 2000, 2200 & 3500 (Marrocco)
Royal Enfield Bullet (Henshaw)
Subaru Impreza (Hobbs)
Sunbeam Alpine (Barker)
Triumph 350 & 500 Twins (Henshaw)
Triumph Bonneville (Henshaw)
Triumph Herald & Vitesse (Ayre)
Triumph Spitfire and GT6 (Ayre)
Triumph Stag (Mort)
Triumph Thunderbird, Trophy & Tiger (Henshaw)
Triumph TR2 & TR3 - All models (including 3A & 3B) 1953 to 1962 (Conners)
Triumph TR4/4A & TR5/250 - All models 1961 to 1968 (Child & Battyll)
Triumph TR6 (Williams)
Triumph TR7 & TR8 (Williams)
Triumph Trident & BSA Rocket III (Rooke)
TVR Chimaera and Griffith (Kitchen)
TVR S-series (Kitchen)
Velocette 350 & 500 Singles 1946 to 1970 (Henshaw)
Vespa Scooters – Classic two-stroke models 1960-2008 (Paxton)
Volkswagen Bus (Copping)
Volkswagen Transporter T4 (1990-2003) (Copping/Cservenka)
VW Golf GTI (Copping)
VW Beetle (Copping)
Volvo 700/900 Series (Beavis)
Volvo P1800/1800S, E & ES 1961 to 1973 (Murray)

Those Were The Days ... Series

Alpine Trials & Rallies 1910-1973 (Pfundner)
American 1/2-ton Pickup Trucks of the 1950s (Mort)
American 1/2-ton Pickup Trucks of the 1960s (Mort)
American 'Independent' Automakers – AMC to Willys 1945 to 1960 (Mort)
American Station Wagons – The Golden Era 1950-1975 (Mort)
American Trucks of the 1950s (Mort)
American Trucks of the 1960s (Mort)
American Woodies 1928-1953 (Mort)
Anglo-American Cars from the 1930s to the 1970s (Mort)
Austerity Motoring (Bobbitt)
Austins, The last real (Peck)
Brighton National Speed Trials (Gardiner)
British and European Trucks of the 1970s (Peck)
British Drag Racing – The early years (Pettitt)
British Lorries of the 1950s (Bobbitt)
British Lorries of the 1960s (Bobbitt)
British Touring Car Racing (Collins)
British Police Cars (Walker)
British Woodies (Peck)
Buick Riviera (Mort)
Café Racer Phenomenon, The (Walker)
Chevrolet½-ton C/K-Series Pickup Trucks 1973-1987 (Mort)
Don Hayter's MGB Story – The birth of the MGB in MG's Abingdon Design & Development Office (Hayter)
Drag Bike Racing in Britain – From the mid '60s to the mid '80s (Lee)
Dune Buggy Phenomenon, The (Hale)
Dune Buggy Phenomenon Volume 2, The (Hale)
Endurance Racing at Silverstone in the 1970s & 1980s (Parker)
Hot Rod & Stock Car Racing in Britain in the 1980s (Neil)
Mercedes-Benz Trucks (Peck)
MG's Abingdon Factory (Moylan)
Motor Racing at Brands Hatch in the Seventies (Parker)
Motor Racing at Brands Hatch in the Eighties (Parker)
Motor Racing at Crystal Palace (Collins)
Motor Racing at Goodwood in the Sixties (Gardiner)
Motor Racing at Nassau in the 1950s & 1960s (O'Neil)
Motor Racing at Oulton Park in the 1960s (McFadyen)
Motor Racing at Oulton Park in the 1970s (McFadyen)
Motor Racing at Thruxton in the 1970s (Grant-Braham)
Motor Racing at Thruxton in the 1980s (Grant-Braham)
Superprix – The Story of Birmingham Motor Race (Page & Collins)
Three Wheelers (Bobbitt)

Great Cars

Austin-Healey – A celebration of the fabulous 'Big' Healey (Piggott)
Jaguar E-type (Thorley)
Jaguar Mark 1 & 2 (Thorley)
Jaguar XK A Celebration of Jaguar's 1950s Classic (Thorley)
Triumph TR – TR2 to 6: The last of the traditional sports cars (Piggott)
Volkswagen Beetle – A Celebration of the World's Most Popular Car (Copping)

www.veloce.co.uk

First published in March 2023, reprinted June 2023 by Veloce Publishing Limited, Veloce House, Parkway Farm Business Park, Middle Farm Way, Poundbury, Dorchester DT1 3AR, England. Tel +44 (0)1305 260068/Fax 01305 250479/e-mail info@veloce.co.uk/web www.veloce.co.uk.
ISBN: 978-1-787115-93-4; UPC: 6-36847-01593-0.
 British Library Cataloguing in Publication Data – A catalogue record for this book is available from the British Library. Typesetting, design and page make-up all by Veloce Publishing Ltd on Apple Mac. Printed and bound by CPI Group (UK) Ltd, Croydon, CR0 4YY.

VAUXHALL CARS

1945 to 1995

A Pictorial History

Trevor Alder

VELOCE

CONTENTS

Introduction

When Veloce approached me to write this volume, I was delighted. Upon looking for source material, I was able to pull from all my previous notes for my 1991 book, *Vauxhall, The Postwar Years*, and utilise a vast archive I have gathered in the 32 years since, thus creating a brand new super volume covering 50 years of the postwar Vauxhall car and (somewhat briefly) the smaller Bedford/Vauxhall van history up until the introduction of the Omega in the mid-1990s.

It's well known that the Vauxhall name came from a busy area in London SE11 and SW8, where in 1903 the Vauxhall Iron Works built its first vehicle, the Vauxhall Light Car, just 5hp and single-cylinder, and offered for 130 guineas (£136 and 10 shillings). An interesting note was the early adoption of the twin bonnet flutes, these used for the final time 79 years later on the run-out 1978-82 Carlton model.

This south bank area in south west London was originally named after a 13th century Luton landowner, one Fulkes de Breaute, whose home was known as Fulkes Hall, a 31-acre site close to the River Thames. The area eventually became known as Fox Hall, then Vauxhall, and it was here that the Vauxhall Iron Works was formed in 1857, a company concentrating on pump and marine paddle steamer engine manufacturing. Its company badge, a heraldic Griffin, was directly taken from Fulkes de Breaute, and is still used today.

Sales took off after the Vauxhall Light Car's public showing at the London Crystal Palace Show in November 1903, and, within two years, fate intervened and the Vauxhall name returned 30 miles north to Luton, where the car manufacturer flourished, soon to produce the 1911 Prince Henry, perhaps Britain's first true sports car. The company grew, and was purchased by General Motors in 1925.

Vauxhall Motors gave substantial help in the Second World War effort by urgently manufacturing thousands of 38-ton Churchill tanks after car production was suspended, with design completed and deliveries being made just nine months after the government order was received. In addition to sundries, a large number of military trucks were also manufactured, as well as fake inflatable cars to fool the opposition into wasting airborne ammunition.

The UK car boom started once the economy began to recover after the war. A huge £14 million expansion programme was embarked on for 1948, with mostly Bedford trucks being built in abundance.

Production initially resumed on most of the previously available cars: first the new L-Type Velox and Wyvern, and then its replacement E-Type using the same model names, joined later by the Cresta. These family cars sold in abundance following extensive marketing and dealership expansion. Several specialist conversions were available over the postwar years; perhaps the most notable from Martin Walter, once one of the biggest employers in Folkestone.

Since then we have seen the introduction of curved glass (largely seen from most manufacturers since the early 1950s), tubeless radial tyres, front and four-wheel-drive transmission, diesel power, turbo-charging, computerised engine management, global shared design strategies and anti-lock brakes. There has also been some success in racing and rallying.

Vauxhall production was also introduced in 1964 with the HA Viva, in a new large facility 150 miles north west at Ellesmere Port, built following the 1960 acquisition of land previously occupied by Hooton airfield (opening in 1917) and the 1800s racecourse at Hooton Hall. Vauxhall also produced trucks at its Dunstable, Bedfordshire plant.

I have fond recollections of riding in and driving the family Vauxhall Victor FB, FC, FEs, Bedford Beagle, Chevette, Cavalier Mk1, Carlton, Viceroy and three Senators, including in Europe in later years. For my father's business, I rode up front as a small child in his Bedford CA, then as a teenager driving myself in the early hours to Spitalfields fruit market in Whitechapel, London, picking up wholesale fruit and vegetables for the family market gardening business in a painfully slow and rather overloaded CF pick-up diesel and our CF Luton. This book has brought back so many memories!

In this volume, we celebrate the cars manufactured between 1945 and 1995. We look at production figures, performance, production changes, conversions, trim and engine derivatives. Also covered are the numerous car-based vans in their respective chapters, with the larger light commercials found in Appendix 3 at the back. The Vauxhall badge began appearing on commercial vehicles from 1990, when the long standing and much respected Bedford name was dropped.

Things have moved on a long way since 1995 with increased foreign competition, duel-fuel gas-powered vehicles, improved aerodynamics, increased service schedules and now even electric plug-in vehicles that are taking Vauxhall well into the future ...

I have met so many interesting people while writing this volume. Thanks must go to Vauxhall Motors from where a lot of archive material originally came; Tim Nevison; enthusiasts John Ankerman, Mario Lindsay, and Edmund Lindsay (all well-known faces within the clubs); local friends and fellow enthusiasts Lindon Lait and Simon Spikesley; and of course my wife, who has seen me hiding behind piles of dusty magazines and brochures for a few months.

Overall it was a pleasure compiling this book, and I have learnt and revisited so much. I do hope the reader finds it of interest.

Trevor Alder
Suffolk, UK
"Vauxhall, once driven, forever smitten"

Note

Concerning technical data: measurements are displayed in imperial with metric units in brackets. All fuel tank capacities are in imperial gallons, and weights are published as unladen; vehicles often had some fuel in the tank, so amounts published should be treated as estimates only. Widths quoted are excluding any mirrors fitted, which might add an extra 5in (127mm) each side.

Over time, the type designations have certainly varied between 'Series' and 'Type.' For this volume the latter has been used, ie E-Type as opposed to E-series.

The author in 2022.

Late 1960s Ventora FD.

Early postwar cars: HIX, HIY, J and L-Types

The immediate prewar scene

The starting point for this book is of course 1945, but it is important to briefly review Vauxhall products from before the Second World War to complete the bigger picture. Essentially as war was declared in September 1939 there were four main models on the production line at Luton: the GY/GL Twenty Five and H-Type Ten (both announced in 1937), and the I-Type Twelve and J-Type Fourteen (both from 1938).

The big 3215cc, six-cylinder, seven-seater Twenty Five was not built after the war, this being the last Vauxhall to be built with a separate chassis. The Ten was a small 1203cc four-cylinder car in saloon and coupé form, and was lengthened and widened for 1940 production and identified with a boot-mounted spare wheel. The similar Twelve had a larger 1442cc four-cylinder engine and had a 7in longer wheelbase than the Ten. The Fourteen was the largest model, with a six-cylinder 1781cc engine.

1939-1945 war years

By May 1940 it became imperative for Vauxhall production to switch to the 38-ton Churchill tank (the design-to-build setup took less than a year), so passenger car production was halted save for a few military staff cars and extensive Bedford truck supply for the war effort. Thus, 250,000 Bedfords were built plus jet engines, 5,000,000 jerrycans, shells, decoy camouflage vehicles and venturi tubes for rocket launchers. The total tank production was 5650 – using nearly a quarter of a million tons of metal – and, when the end of the war was announced, six prototypes for a successor of the Churchill tank were already under test, together with a three-quarter-track military vehicle based on a captured enemy vehicle. Following the end of the Second World War in September 1945, production of passenger cars was slowly reintroduced in 1946 and a total of over 30,000 cars were built throughout 1947. Certainly consumer money was in short supply, coupled with fuel rationing and raw materials including metal for the factory.

Ten, Twelve, Fourteen and vans

Whilst only a handful of the original prewar I-Type Twelves were produced in 1946, production concentrated on an uprated HIY Ten in saloon (with no coupé version now as this was dropped), the HIX Twelve saloon and the 70mph J-Type Fourteen model, of which 30,511 were sold postwar. Essentially, however, these were prewar cars with necessary postwar updates to allow production to continue and the design of the forthcoming 1948 L-Types to be finalised. Due to the continued government export drive at the time, a great deal of these cars were exported, never to be seen again within UK shores, meaning surviving domestic cars are almost non-existent.

Vauxhall Ten.

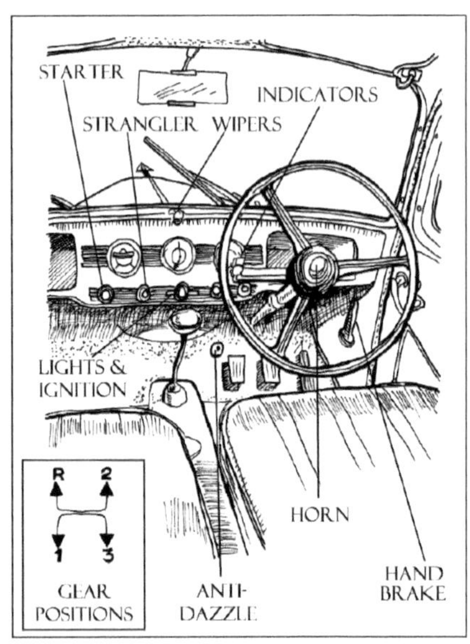

Vauxhall Ten dashboard designation.

Vauxhall Twelve (right) and Fourteen.

1947 press advert inviting customers to a Luton dealer open day: shown here 10/12hp saloon (top) and 14hp saloon.

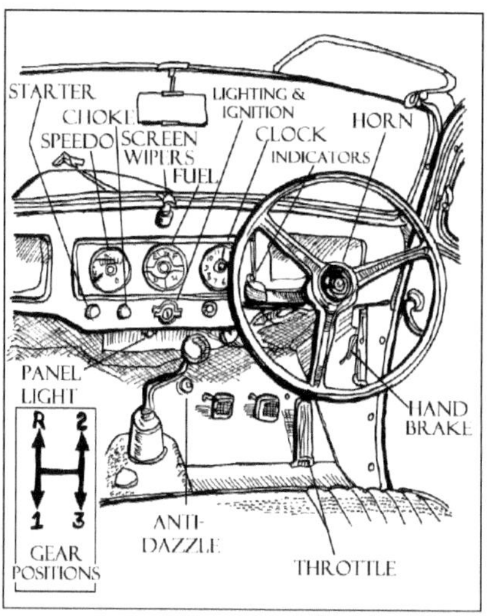

Vauxhall 12hp dashboard designation.

The J-Type 12hp. Postwar cars had horizontal lines on the front grille rather than the previous vertical lines.

The postwar Tens had a 4in longer wheelbase and extra side glass in the rear door, and later 12/4 models adopted the larger 1442cc engine. The small Ten was deleted in 1947 due to a change in the car tax system where a flat rate tax was imposed, making the use of the very slightly smaller engine less attractive.

The H-Type was also available as the Bedford HC, a small 5/6cwt delivery van with 70ft^3 internal capacity. From 1938 the van was produced based on the H 10/4 saloon. Production paused during the war, then resumed from 1946, initially with the 1203cc engine, then later the 1442cc. Vauxhall was proud of its economic running capabilities, and had the RAC conduct a strictly controlled test trial on busy roads with a diminishing load and frequent stops in the busy city rush hour, in which it achieved nearly 41mpg. Van production stopped at L-Type launch time in September 1948, along with the remaining

The Vauxhall J-Type.

HIX-Type 12hp.

Vauxhall J-Type Fourteen, prewar styling still very much evident.

postwar passenger cars. Converted side-glazed versions of the van were manufactured after the war by coachbuilder Martin Walter of Folkestone, which had already produced the splendid Wingham cabriolet based on several models in the Vauxhall range in the 1930s, and which would later become key in Bedford conversions. The converted van also had rear seats, just like the later Bedford Beagle HA.

The bigger HIX Twelve saloon was sold now with horizontal radiator grille bars for £422 and lasted right through until the introduction of the L-Type Wyvern and Velox in 1948. The postwar J-Type Fourteen soldiered on successfully with slight modifications to the facia, with pink instead of green-faced instruments and design changes to the bonnet

Vauxhall I-Type Twelve Four with 102in wheelbase. Very few were produced postwar, possibly just six ...

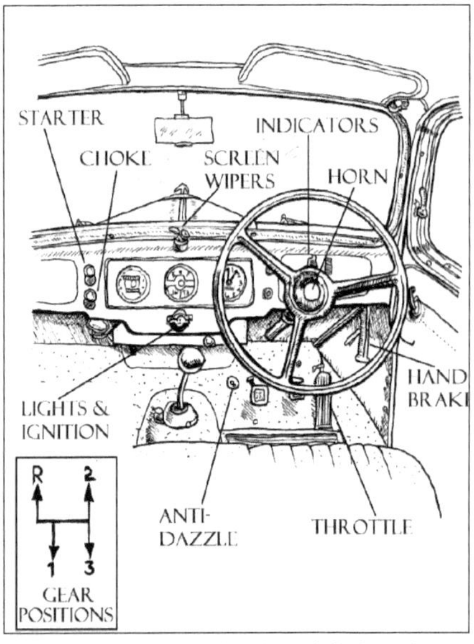

Vauxhall Fourteen dashboard designation, 1948; gear lever still on the floor at this point.

louvres. It sold for £656, was powered by a six-cylinder 1781cc engine, and used an all-synchromesh transmission for its three gears.

The heavier duty 8cwt Bedford JC light van was based on the J-Type saloon. Production began in July 1939 and of course paused during the war years. It was identified by a higher roof-line than the HC van, with a longer wheelbase, too. There were several body-styles of this commercial vehicle sold in Australia.

The two car-based postwar vans that were available, badged as Bedfords (see text).

The JC was replaced by a higher roofed PC van, which was itself retired later in 1952, following the introduction of the much larger CA van. The JC chassis was also used by J-Type cars.

HIX, HIY, J-Type & van media advertising slogans

10-horse sense (Ten)
The cheapest real motoring that money can buy (Ten & Twelve)
Better motoring for less money (Twelve)
Built to save you money (Twelve)
Vauxhall for value (Twelve & Fourteen)
The car that made 14hp motoring famous (Vauxhall Fourteen)
For performance plus economy – choose Vauxhall (New Zealand Ten, Twelve & Fourteen)
40.69mpg under working conditions (Bedford HC van)

HIX, HIY, J-TYPE BODY TYPES: four-door saloon, van (H & J-types), 1946-1947 (Ten), 1946-1948 (12 & 14); **manufactured at**: Luton; **number produced**: 44,047 (Ten & Twelve), 30,511 (Fourteen)
PERFORMANCE: **top speed**: 60mph (100kph) (Ten), 67mph (110kph) (Twelve), 72mph (119kph) (Fourteen); **0-50mph (82kph)** 18 sec (Ten), 19.6 sec (Twelve), 18.4 sec (Fourteen); **average economy**: 35-40mpg (Ten & Twelve), 25-30mpg (Fourteen).
MEASUREMENTS: **length**: 13ft 2in/4.01m (Ten & Twelve), 13ft 11in/4.24m (Fourteen); **width**: 5ft 1in/1.55m (Ten & Twelve), 5ft 4in/1.63m (Fourteen); **height**: 5ft 2in/1.57m (Ten), 5ft 5in/1.65m (Twelve), 5ft 3in/1.60m (Fourteen); **wheelbase**: 8ft 2in/2.49m (Ten & Twelve), 8ft 9in/2.67m (Fourteen); **weight**: 2072lb/940kg (Ten), 2100lb/952kg (Twelve), 2492lb/1130kg (Fourteen); **wheels**: 16in; **turning circle**: 35ft/10.7m (Ten), 38ft 6in/11.73m (Twelve), 42ft/12.8m (Fourteen); **fuel capacity**: 6¾ gallons/30.5 litres (Ten & Twelve), 10 gallons/45.4 litres (Fourteen); **boot capacity**: Advert quote – "Two large suitcases and a smaller case"!
PRICE AT LAUNCH: £371 (Ten & Twelve), £480 (Fourteen), van £140.
TECHNICAL: **engine types**: 1203cc, 1442cc four-cyl, petrol (Ten), 1442cc four-cyl, petrol (Twelve), 1781cc, six-cyl, petrol (Fourteen); **gearbox**: three-speed manual; **suspension**: independent front coil with torsion bars, semi-elliptic rear; **brakes**: drum all round.
TRIM: furniture hide.
KEY OPTIONAL EXTRAS: heater.

L-Type

The L-Type LIX Wyvern and LIP Velox cars were Vauxhall's first new postwar models, and were first shown at the 1948 London Motor Show, mirroring the launch of the new smaller Morris Minor that had been rushed to completion to attend the show, and came some two years ahead of heavy Ford competition, the Mk1 Consul. A first for Vauxhall was a steering column gear change that allowed three-abreast to sit up front in better comfort, albeit in a still rather narrow body. The bodywork was nearly all-new, but the eagle-eyed would note that the door designs were carried over from the previous HIX and HIY models. The headlights were now part of the front wings, rather than fitted externally, creating a fresh modern look up front, with full width front grille, and the rear of the car was redesigned, too. Wheel size was down on previous models from 16 to 15 inches. Overall, the American influence in the styling was obvious.

For the Wyvern, the existing four-cylinder 1442cc engine was used with an emphasis on economy, whilst for the somewhat faster six-cylinder Velox, a brand new 2275cc engine was fitted. Prices were £448 (Wyvern) and £550 (Velox) at launch. The entire Vauxhall range was now upgraded from a 6-volt to 12-volt electrical system, and apart from the cream-coloured wheels used on the Velox (standard body colour was used on the Wyvern) they looked identical from the outside. On the inside, whilst the Velox had leather upholstery, the Wyvern had cloth seat facings and no rear central armrest.

Come and see the new Vauxhalls on stand 148 at the Earl's Court London Motor Show.

Wyvern and Velox model advert with notes on the four new 'Metallichrome' colours.

Wyvern and Velox advert stated 75 per cent of production was for export.

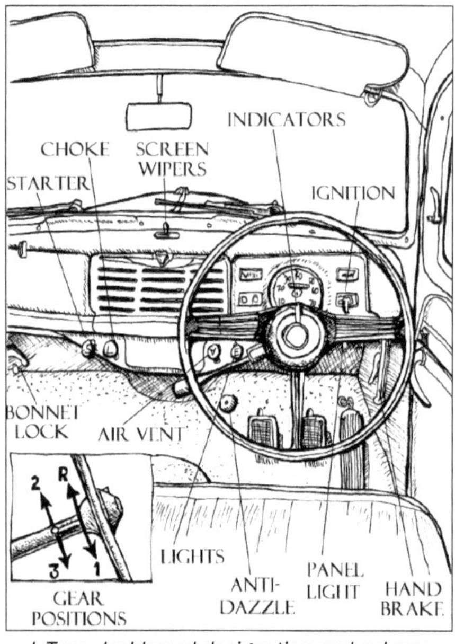

L-Type dashboard designation and column gear change.

One-inch bigger headlamps came in 1949, plus Metallichrome paint option and a parking lamp facility.

By 1950, a 20-acre production building was in use at the Luton facility to keep up with demand, and in May that year UK petrol rationing was discontinued completely, just a couple of years before coupons would allow travel for only 90 miles per month (June 1948), increasing to 180 miles per month (June 1949) unless the red-dye petrol was used – completely illegal in non commercial vehicles, with dire consequences for users and purveyors alike ...

By the end of L-Type production just over 132,000 cars had been made, and the model gave way to the lower profile E-Type in 1952. The last new price (including taxes) of a Wyvern was £647, the Velox £732.

L-Type media advertising slogans

Into 1950 with flying colours

They're new ... and they're news ... these two Vauxhalls ..!

On top ... In top (Velox)

L-TYPE BODY TYPES: four-door saloon, 1948-1951; **manufactured at**: Luton; **number produced**: 55,409 (Wyvern), 76,919 (Velox).
PERFORMANCE: **top speed**: 60mph (100kph) (Wyvern), 74mph (122kph) (Velox); **0-50mph (82kph)**: 27.8 sec (Wyvern), 22.8 sec (Velox); **average economy**: 25-28mpg (Velox), 33-35mpg (Wyvern).
PRICE AT LAUNCH: £448 (Wyvern), £550 (Velox).
MEASUREMENTS: **length**: 13ft 8½in (4.18m); **width**: 5ft 2in (1.57m); **height**: 5ft 5in (1.65m); **wheelbase**: 8ft 1¾in (2.48m); **weight**: 2128lb (965kg) Wyvern, 2352lb (1067kg) Velox; **wheels**: 15in; **turning circle**: 40ft (12.2m); **fuel capacity**: 10 gallons (45.4 litres).
TECHNICAL: **engine types**: 1442cc four-cyl petrol (Wyvern), 2275cc six-cyl petrol (Velox); **gearbox**: three-speed manual; **suspension**: independent front coil & torsion bar, semi-elliptic (rear); **brakes**: drum all round.
TRIM: cloth (Wyvern), leather (Velox).
KEY OPTIONAL EXTRAS: heater.

The new 1948 Vauxhall Wyvern L-Type. Headlamps were now built into the front wings.

The Velox L-Type, defined by its cream-coloured wheels. The doors were brought over from previous bodyshells.

A Wyvern L-Type, with body-coloured wheels. The distinctive bonnet flutes are highlighted clearly in this photograph.

The L-Type Velox. Velox and Wyvern had 'suicide' front doors, opening forwards, as shown here by the double central hinges.

Ten years of Wyvern, Velox and Cresta: E-Types and PAs

E-Type

In the summer of 1951, enter the longer and wider E-Type Wyvern and Velox to replace the earlier four-year-old, rather upright L-Type cars. Following in the tradition of immediate prewar cars, these all-new models (except for having earlier engines at first) were of unitary construction and true five- or even six-seaters. Whilst the Velox was hailed for its 80mph performance, the much slower Wyvern was recognised for its economy. The Vauxhall E-Types literally broke all the moulds; this brand new monocoque design utilised newly available curved glass (an entirely new manufacturing technique) at the Luton plant, which afforded the styling department carte blanche, allowing more modern flowing lines and improved aerodynamics. For example, by 1953 the Morris Minor had been available for three years with a split front windscreen with each section fitted at slightly different angles. By 1956, the Minor had undergone a complete roof redesign, which lost the angle adopted to incorporate the split front screen – an expensive engineering development. Vauxhall was ahead of the crowd with the larger E-Type family saloon, the bodywork all curved to follow the glass from the outset. The four-cylinder Wyvern and six-cylinder Velox looked identical save for their script style badging.

Just the two saloons were offered, with press advertising celebrating hydraulic brakes, entirely new front and rear suspension and within-the-wheelbase seating. The bonnet was hinged on both sides, or for ease of access could be lifted off completely. The prices were certainly higher on the new cars – another £93 to add to the new shape Wyvern, and £70 to the Velox.

In April 1952 it was announced that the E-Type range was to have the newly developed short-stroke 'over square' engines, which had been in the pipeline for several years. These gave longer crankshaft bearing life, extra power and economy and better breathing. The previous engines (1442cc four-cylinder and 2275cc six-cylinder), as used in the L-Types, were dropped; indeed, the earliest Wyvern

Following the discontinued L-Types, the E-Types were available in four-cylinder Wyvern and six-cylinder Velox cars. The Cresta arrived after the mid-1950s face-lift.

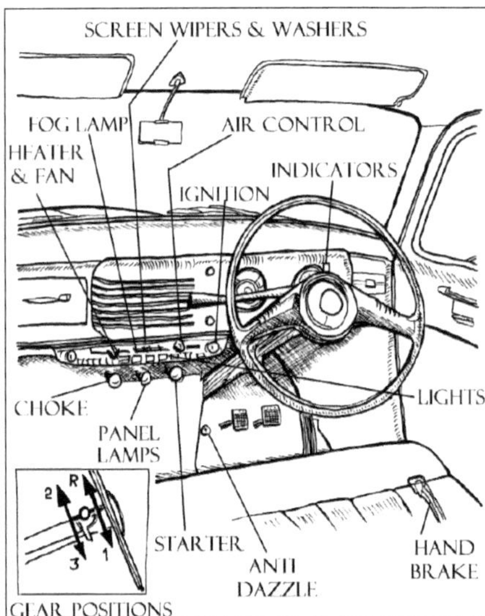

The dashboard designation for the earliest E-Types.

An early E-Type on display at the Vauxhall museum. Note the heavy use of chrome up front.

The rather upright earlier E-Type dashboard.

A 1955 Cresta E-Type in Venezuela.

E-Type Wyvern, Velox and newly available Cresta press advert.

Mid-1950s E-Type Velox.

could attain only 62mph, and just 5313 examples were manufactured. Power output on the new four-cylinder 1508cc was up by 10hp to 45bhp, and on the 2262cc six-cylinder by 11hp to 65bhp. The Wyvern was now good for 70mph, but 0-60mph acceleration still took 37 seconds. A year later, the original side-opening bonnet was replaced by a conventional rear-hinged type, quickly followed by a Vauxhall-approved overdrive conversion kit from GE Neville and Son, Mansfield.

October 1954 saw the introduction of a brand new model, the top-line Cresta, the name used until the demise of the Cresta PC in 1972. This was a deluxe version of the Velox, but finished with two-tone paintwork and interior leather trim, plus a heater, all for £844. Vauxhall's top model, and the factory's first car not fitted with a starting handle, was identified at distance by its white side-wall tyres, and it now shared with the Velox modesty covers over the rear wheels (these also offered to Wyvern models at £2 10s a set). The Cresta utilised the larger six-cylinder engine, with emphasis on driving enjoyment on all its media advertising. At this time, all models gained a lower bonnet line (which in itself was wider), new grilles, smaller half-size bumper over-riders, and refreshed instrumentation inside.

The E-Type went through some further

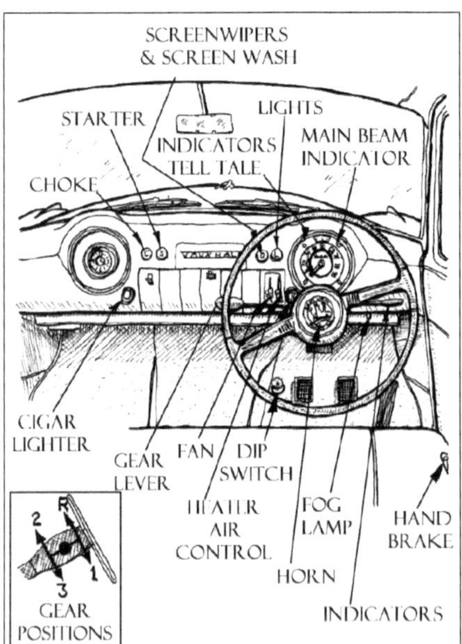

The later style dashboard of the E-Types.

A car with the later dashboard on show in the modern day. (Courtesy Simon Spikesley)

Mid-1950s E-Type Wyvern.

The E-Type Cresta was the top model, note whitewall tyres and rear wheel spats.

changes mid-production in autumn 1955, with deeper front and rear screens (with associated thinner 'A' and 'C' posts to aid visibility), a general tidy up of the chrome trim, and drum braking improvements and door lock enhancements. The door glasses no longer dropped down, but were wound down manually. There were now separate amber rear flashers fitted.

Final model end improvements occurred in October 1956, with electric wipers replacing the earlier camshaft driven type, new attractive colour schemes, and the Cresta had a more restrained two-tone colour scheme, the second colour now reduced to a flash along the body-sides, whilst the rest of the body was just one colour.

In Australia, the Vauxhall E-Types were built locally at the GM facility. The Ute (10cwt pick-up), a woody estate, and the 1952-1955 Vagabond (an attractive two-door convertible) were sold alongside the Velox and Wyvern, as seen with the previous L-Type convertible series in the late 1940s.

Martin Walter had been conveying used E-Types for keen customers at its facility

A later E-Type Velox wears rear wheel spats, as seen on the Cresta.

A two-tone Dormobile estate Velox by Martin Walter, advertised new for £1112.17s including purchase tax. Note the CA pick-up truck behind, with its hinged doors.

in Utilicon Works in Folkestone. These conversions were usually two-tone with the contrasting colour starting just below the window line. In 1957, the Martin Walter Velox Dormobile estate conversion obtained Vauxhall factory blessing, and brand new cars were thus now converted, with the colour division following the swage line halfway down the doors and along. This model was so much more than what the contemporary 'woody' estates of the time had been, and stood apart from the competition. The body lines of the existing saloon shell were cleverly utilised to form an attractive estate body, using fibre-glass reinforced plastics in construction. The tailgate was plastic and top hinged and a tent could be affixed to the rear for camping: advertising claimed using it as a double bed was all the rage when camping ... Conversions to existing cars were still available for at £185.

Another conversion offered at the same

time was from the Grosvenor Carriage Company in Kimberley Road, NW6, London, then later Chaul End, Luton. Rear springs were uprated and it had a handy split opening tailgate (à la the 1970 Range Rover) and curious 'V' pillars behind the rear side doors. Inside it was fully trimmed with a rear floor finished in oak-faced plywood with polished aluminium wearing strips. This all-steel type conversion was also available on a used car for £230 which included a complete respray and weighed 98lb heavier than the saloons. Both these conversions looked completely different, but still retained the original factory lines. Grosvenor had also produced a lesser known woody-style E-Type estate conversion in 1953; the rear section did not slope down and thus the interior cargo area was bigger.

E-Type production slowed in January 1957 in readiness for the new PA range of six-cylinder cars due that autumn. The brand new F-Type Victor took over from the four-cylinder Wyvern in March 1957, bringing back more than one basic body style to Vauxhall's new car line-up, the first time in nearly ten years. Late modifications to the Velox and Cresta E-Type cars involved further refinements to engines, and synchromesh was also fitted to first gear on all gearboxes, which were to be used in the forthcoming PA cars later that year.

E-Type media advertising slogans

Years ahead in engineering leadership
Last word for the ladies! That's Vauxhall value!
All eyes on the big Vauxhalls
Spacious ... Powerful ... Economical! That's Vauxhall value
So far ... for so little, that's Vauxhall value!
... the new car you'll enjoy is a Vauxhall (Cresta)
The sparkling new Cresta (Cresta)
On top ... in top! That's Vauxhall value! (Velox)
The wind's behind you in a Vauxhall
Vauxhall value! Greater than ever for 1956 (Cresta)
For town and country (Grosvenor estate)
Drive where you like, sleep where you like. It's all here (Dormobile estate)
Drive it in company ... drive it alone ... the new car you'll enjoy is a Vauxhall (Cresta)

E-TYPE BODY TYPES: four-door saloons, three independent five-door estates: 1951-1957; **manufactured at**: Luton; **number produced**: 110,588 (Wyvern), 235,296 (Cresta/Velox).
PERFORMANCE: **top speed**: 62-86mph (100-138kph) (early Wyvern/Cresta); **0-60mph (100kph):** 21 sec; **average economy**: 33-35mpg (Wyvern), 25-28mpg (Velox).
PRICE AT LAUCH: £740 (Wyvern), £802 (Velox), £981 (later Cresta).
MEASUREMENTS: **length**: 14ft 4in (4.37m); **width**: 5ft 7in (1.7m); **height**: 5ft 3in (1.6m); **wheelbase**: 9ft 7in (3.83m); **weight**: 2206-2475lb (1000-1122kg); **wheels**: 15in; **turning circle**: 35ft (10.7m); **fuel capacity**: 11 gallons (50 litres).
TECHNICAL: **engine types**: 1442-1508cc four-cyl, 2275-2262cc six-cyl, all petrol; **gearbox**: three-speed manual; **suspension**: independent coil with wishbone front, semi-elliptic rear; **brakes**: drum front and rear.
TRIM: Vynide, Tygan or Elastofab.
KEY OPTIONAL EXTRAS: (1954) high compression cylinder head (7.3:1), rear wheel cover panels, fog lamps, radio, reversing lamps, exhaust deflector, petrol filler lock.

Cresta and Velox PA

Two new model ranges in just one season! Eight months after the introduction of the new Victor F in February 1957, the new Cresta and Velox PA models were announced. These bigger, longer and lower cars were handsome in their transcontinental looks, with one clean unbroken line running from headlamp to tail and use of pronounced tail fins similar to the US Buick Special. Indeed, these lines subtly formed the traditional Vauxhall flutes first introduced on all company products in Edwardian times, albeit then on the bonnet. Front windscreens were Triplex wrap-round (with single-piece rear wrap-round from summer 1959) which gave almost unrivalled panoramic visibility. The PA turning circle was 2ft less than its predecessor, and the interior space was improved partly thanks to an extra two inches in the wheelbase compared to previous E-Types.

The new models made their debut at the

This is the early grille PA.

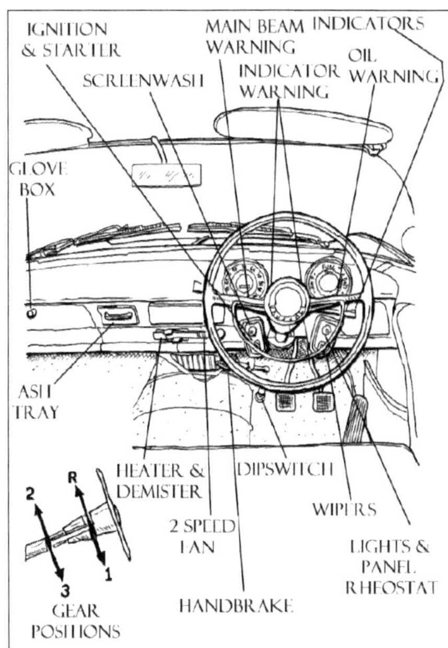

Earlier PA dashboard designation.

An early dashboard with twin 'clocks.' (Courtesy Simon Spikesley)

1957 London Motor Show, and were available in several vibrant colours including pink, a firm favourite with some enthusiasts to this day. Heaters were standardised across the range, and, once again, the gearlever and handbrake were column-mounted so a front bench could be used to seat three abreast. The top Cresta model was offered with white side-wall tyres again, and five two-tone paint schemes (the second colour was applied to the roof and rear deck), although some cars were of single colour. A distinctive see-through circular Griffin badge stood proudly mounted on the top of a chrome strip in the centre of the bonnet on Cresta models, not seen on the cheaper Velox. The stainless steel above the waistline on the Cresta was polished, whereas it was body colour on the Velox, and matching hubcaps were fitted to Cresta, the Velox got chrome. Both models utilised twin round-hooded instrument binnacles.

The new estate from Friary Motors

Early PA cars had a three-piece rear screen.

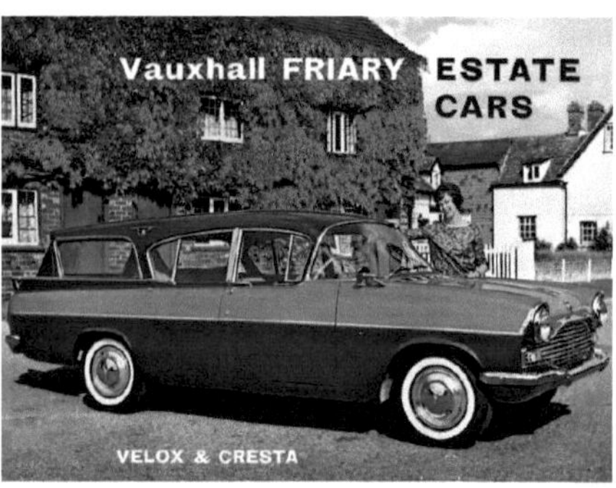

The Friary PA estate conversion brochure cover.

A late 1959 2.2-litre Velox in candy floss pink: always a very sought-after colour.

Tail fins from the 1959 Velox with built-in indicators.

The rear door opening buttons on the PA cars were a bit of a stretch for those with small hands.

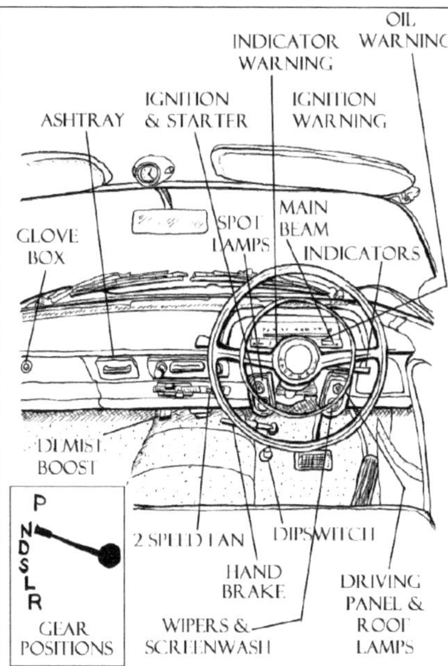

Later PA dashboard designation.

of Basingstoke – one of the best-looking conversions ever in the author's opinion – was available from May 1959. The luggage capacity increased from 30 to 52ft^3 with the rear seats down, and, with no fibre-glass used in its construction, these heavier cars were of all-steel construction. For maximum luggage area, larger capacity twin fuel tanks had to be used and were mounted each side of the spare wheel under the rear floor. The floor and the sides of the luggage compartment were lined with foam-backed Armoride. Underneath, there was uprated semi-elliptic rear suspension, which, whilst giving a firmer ride when unladen, could constitute some extra weight. The estate's overall road footprint was exactly the same as the saloons. The self-propping lift-up lockable tailgate opened to 120 degrees and the trailer wiring was through the vehicle's number plate wiring, and when open, the number plate light illuminated the interior.

Very few conversions existed on the pre face-lift phase of PA cars described here, but there were at least three road tests of these performed by different UK magazines.

The later PA strip speedometer (Courtesy Simon Spikesley).

Cresta PA estate; a later model as used in the royal household. This imperial green car still exists within the Sandringham estate collection and is fitted with fishing rod holders on the roof ...

Friary estates were priced at £1222 (Velox) and £1309 (Cresta). One such early Velox conversion was driven by *Autocar* magazine in 1959 right across Europe to (then) Dubrovnik, Yugoslavia, on an epic, excitingly different and rather adventurous 3071-mile camping trip. Five people and their luggage travelled, and the whole outfit weighed almost two tons with extra petrol etc. Luggage was over double the permissible 8cwt, and they were often driving on unmade roads. Registered 446HPJ, the car suffered from tailgate fixture issues, rattling free and letting in dust in 110°F heat. Word made it back to Basingstoke, which then modified ongoing production examples. Overall, the team achieved 20.8mpg. At one point the travellers had their passports retained by the local police and were fined £8 for camping illegally!

By the end of 1958 wider front quarter-light windows by $1\frac{1}{4}$in had been introduced, which helped improve wind noise at higher speed, and an attractive set of chrome wing mirrors (to be mounted at the windscreen end of the front wings) could be ordered as an official option.

August 1959 saw a larger rounded at top front grille (hiding the new larger radiator) fitted across the range. Up front, the Cresta's stand up Griffin badge was replaced by a less obtrusive bonnet-mounted motif and the two longitudinal raised seam lines on the roof were deleted, this achieved by adding more strength in the 'C' pillars instead. These ran backwards between the three-piece rear window which was also deleted replaced by a one piece curved unit to match the front. Around this time, the flutes on the front wings were discontinued, replaced by straight chrome side mouldings.

In August 1960, the six-cylinder engine was uprated, and its displacement increased from 2262cc to 2651cc, increasing power output by 31hp over the previous 13-year-old engine type which dated back to 1947, giving rise to improved performance. The clutch size was increased, but for automatic fans, the new US Hydra-Matic gearbox became a £170 option from this time adding 15 per cent to its list price. Road wheels were increased from 13in to 14in which allowed more room for the larger brakes.

1960 styling enhancements included front flashers and side lights in neat rectangular units (flashers were now on the inner edges), the boot nameplate incorporated a push button lock plus revised and reshaped rear bumpers now mounted higher. Above this, the distinctive large oval rear lamps were redesigned, replaced by shallower units and the indicators relocated down into them, off the tail fins which now carried a large 'V' motif on their

A 1962 Hydra-Matic PA Cresta draws an admiring look at a Felixstowe classic car event.

rearmost sides. Make no mistake, this was still a Vauxhall ...

For the interior, the fascia now had a full redesign, with a new padded top and horizontal magic strip speedometer: drive below 30mph and it displayed green, amber for 30-60mph and red for above 60mph. One way to keep the speedometer in the red sector was to drive on the new M6 or M1 motorways that had just been opened. The cars could potentially over-rev for long distances here and possibly overheat, and, going forwards, the UK road infrastructure was rapidly becoming more high speed. Thus from February that year, the option of a Laycock de Normanville overdrive became available. The extra gears were available in second for acceleration and top gear for saving fuel on long runs and keeping the engine speed down. Another option, assuming these heavy cars needed to stop quickly from high speed, was that of Lockheed servo-assisted power brakes with larger 10½in discs, offered from July that year just ahead of the new engines.

Further new colours were offered in September 1961, taking the total available to 15 for the Cresta and eight two-tone (14 monotone for the cheaper Velox). Individual front seats became optional; the column gearshift was to remain, however, on such models. An ashtray was fitted on the rear of each seat. Wood cappings were added to fascias and door panels. The front screen wipers (always two-speed) now overlapped in operation, with swept length increased from 11 to 14in.

In the 20th May 1962 edition of the *Sunday Pictorial*, World Champion racing driver Jack Brabham said of the Velox: “This car is as virile as they come ... I couldn’t fault it. It is a good, sound, solid job that proved itself to me thoroughly in comfort, styling and roadholding.” Vauxhall used this keenly in its marketing shortly before production ended and made way for the PB cars in October 1962. In Australia, however, the PA was available until as late as 1965, having first arrived there in May 1958.

Very few PA models still exist, and estates are even rarer. A lot were heavily customised in the 1960s and 1970s and gained a ‘rock ’n’ roll’ image. Indeed, Coventry Motor Museum houses the PA used in the *Ghost Town* music video, made by The Specials.

The rear of a late model 1962 2.6-litre PA. Note the V motifs on the rear fins.

The rear end of an early PA. The back lights are visibly taller, and the two-tone treatment is clearly different compared with the previous picture.

PA media advertising slogans

People going places go Vauxhall (Cresta)
Everyone drives better in a Vauxhall (Cresta)
Go ahead people go Vauxhall (Cresta)
Marvellous new cars these 1960s Vauxhalls (Cresta)
Good looks make good sense (Cresta)
As virile as they come (Velox)
Skittles anyone? (Friary)
Very distinguished motoring (Cresta)
Very distinguished estate car (Friary)
Built for the motorway age

PA BODY TYPES: four-door saloon, five-door estate (conversion): 1957-1962; **manufactured at**: Luton; **number produced**: 81,841 (1957-1960), 91,923 (1960-1962).
PERFORMANCE: **top speed**: 90mph (145kph); **0-60mph (100kph)** 17 sec; **average economy**: 19-26mpg.
PRICE AT LAUCH: £983 (Velox), £1073 (Cresta).
MEASUREMENTS: **length**: 14ft 10in (4.52m); **width**: 5ft 8in (1.72m); **height**: 4ft 9in (1.48m); **wheelbase**: 8ft 9.25in (2.67m); **weight**: 2623lb (1190kg); **wheels**: 13in & 14in; **turning circle**: 37ft 4in (11.4m); **fuel capacity**: 10.5 gallons (48 litres) saloon & 14 gallons (64 litres) Friary estate; **boot capacity**: 30/52ft^3 on estate (seats up/down).
TECHNICAL: **engine types**: 2262-2651cc, six-cyl, petrol (shared with Bedford trucks); **gearbox**: three-speed manual, three-speed automatic; **suspension**: independent coil with wishbone front, semi-elliptic rear; **brakes**: drum all round.
TRIM: Vynide or Tygan Rayon.
KEY OPTIONAL EXTRAS: Hydra-Matic auto, overdrive (February 1960), radio, fog lamps, reversing light, exterior mirrors and locking fuel flap, front central armrest (Velox).

Twenty years of Victors, Ventoras and VXs: The F, FB, FC, FD and FEs

Victor F-Type

By the mid-1950s, to compliment their larger models, rival UK companies Ford, Rootes and BMC had more than one alternative body style with their fast-selling economy Anglias, Minxs and Riley/Wolseley 1500s. Just ahead of the launch of the E-Type Cresta cars in 1954, Vauxhall initiated the design of a completely new smaller model, the Victor F. Prototypes were running by October that year, and after gearing up, full production started in February 1957, just in time for the Victor F-Type to be displayed at the Geneva Motor Show in Switzerland the following month.

For power, the existing four-cylinder 1508cc Wyvern overhead valve engine was modified: the cylinder block was deepened, it was made stronger, and was now rated at 55hp, 15hp more than when fitted in the Wyvern. The three-speed gearbox was now all-synchromesh.

The Victor saloon derivative was launched first, cost was £729, and the Super priced at £758. This plusher model came with door armrests, brighter trim-work, a rear ashtray, and a rather novel idea of the exhaust running through one side of the rear bumper. Its performance was up on the Wyvern, which was now discontinued, leaving just the E-Type Cresta running. Top speed for this lower-bodied Victor was 75mph (the Wyvern was around 70mph), and 0-60mph was six seconds quicker at 15.5 seconds. The *Sunday Times* newspaper test reported: "It goes along twisty roads almost like a little sports car." Overall, the USA-inspired styling was well received, and the dog-leg 'A' post was also soon adopted on the PA cars late in 1957.

A rather well-styled estate became available a year later. This was the first ever in-house Vauxhall estate produced; previous such models always being conversions by outside firms. Heavy marketing of the estate followed, with colour adverts appearing on the front of weekly motoring magazines. "Own a wonderful world!" stated one tag line, with happy families depicted in beach scenes with their estates.

An early Victor F press advert: just visible are the sculptured rear doors.

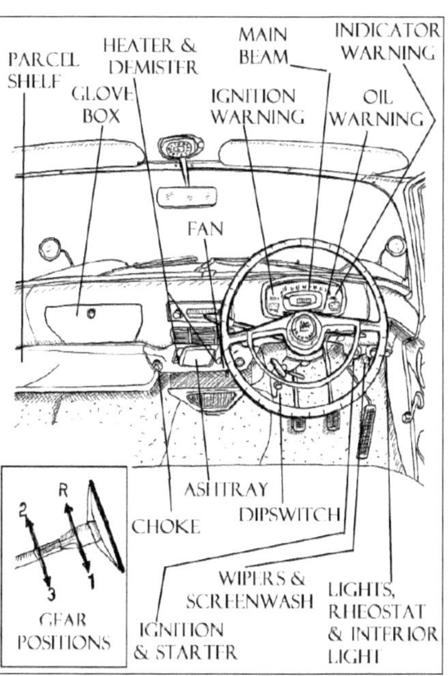

The earlier Victor F dashboard layout.

Twin central bonnet ridges seen on the earlier Victor Fs.

The tailgate was a flip-up hinged type, and internal boot capacity with the rear seats down was 45½ft³.

By September 1958, the Series 2 Victor F-Type had arrived. Plainer bumpers were fitted, and the Super's exhaust lost its aforementioned novel exit through the chrome bumper. These models were also identified by the lack of bright-work on the side window

The 'A' post windscreen reverse rake is really evident here on this early dashboard Victor F. (Courtesy Simon Spikesley)

Press advertising on a phase 2 Victor F estate. So many ads up to this time were painted images, with photographic representation coming in from the early 1960s.

The same car seen speeding towards Felixstowe, Suffolk, in 2019.

Phase 2 Victor F saloon and estate for the export market.

Phase 2 Victor F dashboard photographed in 2022. (Courtesy Simon Spikesley)

surrounds. The rear doors lost their sculpture-style feature and the bonnet had a single north-south crease, no longer twin (see photo). A plusher Victor deluxe was added to the range, with individual front seats and featured leather seating all round.

Final revisions were made in August 1960, with a noticeably deeper rear screen and vertical flutes added to the boot-lid. A brand new facia and revised five-bar front grille completed the look. This later model continued for 11 months before the factory summer break in July 1961, when production stopped. Over 390,000 were manufactured 1957-1961, with around two thirds of these exported, much to the delight of the postwar export drive. Very few survive today often due to early corrosion problems encountered.

F-Type media advertising slogans
Pick of the bunch
Salute the Victor
Drive into the motorway age
Everyone drives better in a Vauxhall (Series 2)
Goodness spacious. What a wonderful Vauxhall this is (estate)
Vauxhall economy makes this wagon a pleasure! (estate)
Own a wonderful world! Own a Vauxhall (estate)
Likes road, loves luggage! (estate)

F-TYPE BODY TYPES: four-door saloon, five-door estate, 1957-1961; **manufactured at**: Luton; **number produced**: 390,745.
PERFORMANCE: **top speed**: 75mph (120kph); **0-60mph (100kph)**: 28 seconds; **average economy**: 30mpg.
PRICE AT LAUNCH: £729 (standard), £759 (Super)
MEASUREMENTS: **length**: 13ft 11in (4.24m); **width**: 5ft 2¼in (1.58m); **height**: 4ft 10.25in (1.48m); **wheelbase**: 8ft 2in (2.49m); **turning circle**: 34ft 6in (10.5m); **weight**: 2700lb (1224kg); **wheels**: 13in; **fuel tank capacity**: 7.5 gallons (34 litres); **boot capacity**: 19ft^3.
TECHNICAL: **engine types**: 1508cc, four-cyl, petrol; **gearbox**: three-speed manual & 'two-pedal control'; **suspension**: independent wishbone with coil (front), rigid axle, semi-elliptic (rear); **brakes**: drum all round.
TRIM: Vynide, leather.
KEY OPTIONAL EXTRAS: radio, heater, fog lamps, clock, screen washer.

Victor and VX4/90 FB

Almost from the outset in October 1961, there were four Victor FBs: saloon and estate in Super form and top of the range deluxe (with leather seats), quickly followed four weeks later by the (as badged) 'VX Four-Ninety,' later badged just as the VX4/90. The estate version again was built at Luton and not outsourced. At the 1961 London Motor Show at Earl's Court, the Victor won two gold medals for its coachwork from the Institute of British Carriage and Automobile Manufacturers, with Vauxhall advertising extolling "The clean line of good design."

A lot of effort had been made to improve the manufacturing process after many complaints about corrosion on the original Victor F models, and the FBs had virtually no horizontal surfaces, visible or invisible, for water to collect

The VX4/90 was the first sporting car that Vauxhall had produced since the 30/98 decades earlier, and it did not disappoint. With snazzier colour options, the two-tone scheme was added to the body flanks, whereas on the Victor the roof was the different colour. The £971 VX4/90 was the first sporty Vauxhall to have a painted red engine block, something that still continued later on with the 'hotter' versions of Vauxhalls. Although the (blue, grey, black and cherry red) seats were available in vinyl only, the rear was sculptured for two occupants with a central armrest and the driver had a rev counter. The dashboard and door cards included extensive use of wood, and there were map pockets on the front doors. Outside, the rear lamp clusters were unique with extended bezels traveling up the rear wings, although some export FB 'Sherwood' estate cars featured these, too. There were front disc brakes and an all-synchromesh gearbox. The many press adverts called it "The velvet touch," with racing driver Reg Parnell praising his own VX4/90. The result? It was an instant sales success. It was certainly faster than its Victor sister cars, with *Practical Motorist* magazine recording a top speed of 89.9mph and 0-60mph 16.4 seconds in its October 1962 issue. The two-tone paints were simplified a year later on the VX4/90, losing the step-up look on the rear doors and gaining a square number plate on the boot lid.

An early series Victor FB saloon at an Ipswich gathering in around 2019.

A Victor FB estate with two-tone coachwork. Note continued use of saloon rear lamps.

A face-lifted Victor FB from 1964. The Luton number plate was still pre 'A' or 'B' registered, as some areas took a while to catch up with the new system, which was fully implemented across all areas at 'C' registration (1965).

The VX Four-Ninety FB in its earlier guise. Unusually, the two-tone treatment on this very early car was extended over the fuel flap, unlike on production cars.

A later 1964 FB VX4/90. Note the change in shape of the side 'spear.'

In the autumn of 1963, FD engine displacement was increased from 1508cc to 1594cc using the same stroke but a greater bore. This added an extra 13hp on the Victors, and took the VX4/90 to 86hp.

In the FB's final year of production, a distinctive anodised aluminium front grille replaced the earlier type, plus the deluxe models now had wood trim on the facia and newly designed front seats. The two chrome strips at the bottom of the saloon's boot panel had by now been deleted as were the Victor's large wing badges. There were not many conversions offered, but worthy of note was the Martin Walter ambulance conversion on the estate and from Acton, west London, the LawrenceTune bolt-on kit for the VX4/90, which shaved off two seconds from the 0-60mph time and gave an easy top speed capability of 90mph. The December 1962 *Practical Motorist* road test stated "Bearing in mind that this bolt on conversion consists of only a replacement carburettor, inlet and exhaust manifolds, the improvement in performance and flexibility is impressive."

FB media advertising slogans

The clean line of good design is doing fine
Good design speaks for itself – and for you
Hello stranger!
Let's take my car (face-lift)
Vivid motoring with the velvet touch (VX4/90)
The velvet touch ... at both ends of the clock (VX4/90)
More vivid! More velvet! - with the new, bigger engine (VX4/90)
Go on then – drive, the VX4/90 understands (VX4/90 face-lift)

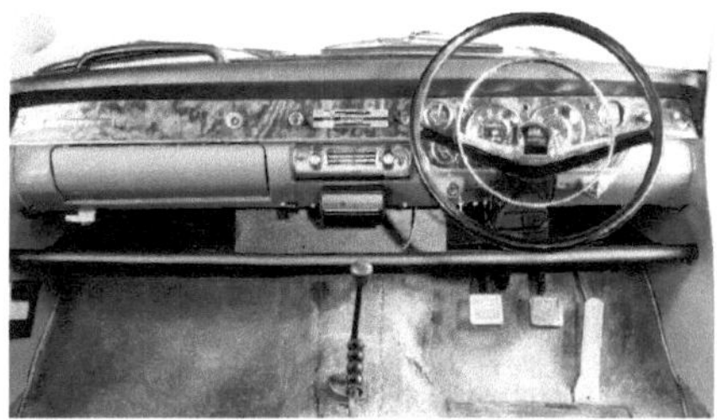

1964 season VX4/90 FB dashboard with its extra instrumentation over and above the lower model Victor. The control knobs had been repositioned, as they were previously hard for the driver to reach if belted up.

FB BODY TYPES: four-door saloon, five-door estate, 1961-1964; **manufactured at**: Luton; **number produced**: 328,640 (all FB).
PERFORMANCE: **Victor top speed**: 77mph (124kph); **0-60mph (100kph)**: 23.4 sec; **average economy**: 28mpg.
PRICE ON LAUNCH: £745-£861 (Victors), £814 (VX4/90).
MEASUREMENTS: **length**: 14ft 5in (4.4m); **width**: 5ft 4in 1.63m); **height**: 4ft 8in (1.42m); **wheelbase**: 8ft 4in (2.54m); **weight**: 2212lb (1003kg); **wheels**: 14in; **turning circle**: 33ft 3in (10.13m); **fuel capacity**: 10 gallons (45 litres); **boot capacity**: 21½ft³.
TECHNICAL: **engine types**: 1508, 1594cc, four-cyl petrol; **suspension**: coil springs/wishbone (front), live axle, half-elliptic (rear); **gearbox**: three-speed, four-speed manual; **brakes**: drum front & rear.
TRIM: vinyl, leather.
KEY OPTIONAL EXTRAS: two-tone paint, four-speed all-synchro gearbox, heater, screen washer, fog lamps, safety belts, mirrors.

Victor and VX4/90 FC (101)

The softer, rounder lines of the new '101' FC range of Victors and VX4/90s were first publicly displayed at the 1964 UK Motor Show. As with previous Victors, a four-door saloon and five-door estate were produced on base model, then Super, then (top model) deluxe platforms like the previous FB, and the emphasis that year was on improved space. The FC 101 had a concave back window and the side glass now took on a pronounced curve (soon adopted by the new range of PC cars); arguably better-looking and more modern than the contemporary Mk1 Ford Cortinas and Hillman Minx. The new range sold well, contributing to a company profit of over £17 million in 1964.

Again, the so-called "Clean cut, sleek and racy" twin carburettor VX4/90 was higher specified and came with flashier wheel trims and front grille, chrome-bordered side flashes with an alternative colour, bucket seats, and better instrumentation once again (amps, volts, rev counter in addition to all the normal gauges), and in the end 6 per cent of overall sales of the FC were VX4/90s, which was 18 per cent more expensive than the Super deluxe. Just like the hotter Viva HA cars, the rear lamps had their own unique appearance, each function getting its own chrome surround cluster.

In August of 1966, Victor models received the almost obligatory end of line grille revision. The individual letters that spelt out 'VAUXHALL' on the bonnet's leading edge were deleted, and the manufacturer's name was now incorporated into the new grille, which in turn received two vertical style lines to continue down from those seen on the bonnet. Individual boot badging was not so affected, but the Victor badges on the leading edges of the front wings were deleted. Engine bhp was increased from 70 to 76 as the compression ratio was increased from 8:.5:1 to 9:1, and the faster, four-speed-only (with floor-mounted stick shift) VX4/90 was now a giddy 81hp and gained a company first: a limited-slip differential for the back axle. It could achieve around 90mph flat out, around 10mph faster than the Victors. However, *Popular Motoring*, a UK magazine, recorded a 0-60mph acceleration figure of 17.8 seconds and top speed of 85mph in a special fold-out report in its July 1967 issue.

In May 1967, *Autocar* magazine sneaked a late road test of the revised 101 deluxe saloon, and approved of the car, save for some

The Victor FC 101 saloon, the de luxe model with chrome wheel covers and extra bright-work below the window line and fully extending down each side of the car.

A very late 101 saloon with the later grille.

Picnic time with a pair of face-lifted 101 estates!

A 1965 FC VX4/90 on a new UK motorway.

niggles: "The inverted-vee capping piece along the top of each wing is crudely finished off where it meets the roof gutter. Also the front grille is awkward to wash, having sharp edges which catch on sponge or cloth. .." By October 1967 the 101s were discontinued in favour of the new Coke-bottle shape FDs.

FC (101) media advertising slogans

Bred for success, better than ever for '66

When a car looks this good, you like to keep it where you can see it

Now the space-making Victor 101 heads the Vauxhall range

The versatile Victor 101 estate car

Exciting way to find the sun – Vauxhall Victor 101

Clean cut, sleek and racy (VX4/90)

Welcome to the Club Exclusive (VX4/90)

FC BODY TYPES: four-door saloon, five-door estate: 1964-1967; **manufactured at**: Luton; **number produced**: 219,894 (Victor), 13,449 (VX4/90).

PERFORMANCE: **0-60mph (100kph)**: 28.5 & 17.8 sec (Victor & VX490); **top speed**: 81-85mph (130-136kph) (Victor/VX4/90); **average economy**: 24mpg.

PRICE AT LAUNCH: £678 (base model), £871 (VX4/90).

MEASUREMENTS: **length**: 14ft 9in (4.49m); **width**: 5ft 4¾in (1.64m); **height**: 4ft 8½in (1.44m); **wheelbase**: 8ft 4in (2.54m); **weight**: 2316lb (1051kg); **wheels**: 16in; **turning circle**: 32ft 4in; **fuel capacity**: 10.1 gallons (45.9 litres); **boot capacity**: 23ft^3.

TECHNICAL: **engine types**: 1595cc four-cyl, petrol; **gearbox**: three- & four-speed manual, automatic; **suspension**: independent coil with wishbone (front), live axle half-elliptic leaf

The FC VX4/90 was the sporty Vauxhall of the day.

Extra instrumentation shown as fitted to this export VX4/90.

(rear); **gearbox**: three- & four-speed manual, automatic; **brakes**: drum all round, optional front disc.
TRIM: Ambla.
KEY OPTIONAL EXTRAS: four-speed gears with floor change, automatic, leather seats, oversize tyres.

Victor, Ventora and VX4/90 FD

The London Motor Show 1967, and this year the FDs made their bold introduction. "The great '68 symbol ... Sleek, scorchy new Victor," proclaimed the advertising, with carefully chosen colour images of the new Coke-bottle shaped cars kicking up desert dust at speed, in this era of machismo on opposite lock ... The Victors were back again, bigger and faster with new slant-four engines of 1599cc and 1975cc in four-door saloon form – but with the five-door estate, as with previous models, customers had to wait until the following May for their 60ft^3 capacity car.

The styling was bold, with particularly thin windscreen pillars and four headlamps up front, and the model was awarded the Don Safety Trophy for its contribution to road safety. *The Times* newspaper stated it was "The Star of the Show." Both manual four-speed and three-speed automatic transmissions were available, the only common parts carried over from the previous FC cars. The 1600 had bench seats and a column gear change again, with the 2-litre having separate front seats. The model lasted longer than its predecessors – four and a half years, partly due to the design studio working hard on the new Viva, Firenzas and Bedford CF vans.

Top line designation went to the new £1101 Ventora from spring of 1968, which utilised the ex Chevrolet six-cylinder 3294cc unit also previously seen in less tuneful states in some larger Bedford trucks. This new Ventora was dubbed 'The Lazy Fireball' due to its under-worked engine, which provided 123hp and gave the Ventora a top speed of just over 100mph and 0-60 time of 11.8 seconds. Identified by a smart vinyl roof, flashier wheel trims and four headlamps, its high fuel consumption was its downfall, whilst the Victors were good for 20-22mpg, Ventora was tested with just 18mpg as a test car average. A six-cylinder estate was also sold with Ventora grille, but oddly this was badged as a Victor. October 1969 saw the 1600s becoming the SL, and the 2-litre become the Super. At this point enter an updated Ventora II, which replaced the earlier model, and with an increase in overall gearing 106mph was

The Coke-bottle shape Victor FD saloon.

An FD Victor 2000 estate at the Luton works. A 1600 could also be purchased.

Interior of a Victor 2000 FD with wooden facia and individual front seats.

The Ventora FD from 1970. This model came with a fashionable vinyl roof.

The Victor FD estate with optional 3.3-litre six-cylinder engine. This model utilised the Ventora grille and wheel trims.

now achievable. Seating was better, the fronts reclined and the rears were now sculptured. The rather out of date two-speed Powerglide transmission was replaced by the modern three-speed Strasbourg automatic gearbox, and reversing lights were standardised.

Also in October 1969 the faster, higher specification VX4/90 was announced at the Paris Motor Show (this slightly ahead of Earl's Court). It was fitted with the same twin carburettor 1979cc engine as the Viva GT, and over 14,000 were produced in its 24-month production run, the last of the Ventoras selling for £1564. Media advertising on the VX4/90 model was minimal, with concentration on Victor and Ventora models.

FD media advertising slogans

The great '68 symbol. Sleek, scorchy new Victor
Two lively litres give a gripping performance
Get Victor power. Go horizon hunting
It's the four wheel limpet
And you feel trailblazer
The inside story of out and out luxury
We test prototypes to destruction and production models to perfection
Pack up. Move out. In style (estate)
Performance-plus (VX4/90)
The lazy fireball (Ventora)
When you've got this much power you can take things easily (Ventora)
Mighty Ventora. Where luxury meets power (Ventora)
The Vauxhall breeds got style (Ventora)

FD BODY TYPES: four-door saloon, five-door estate: 1967-1972; **manufactured at**: Luton; **number produced**: 198,085 FDs (incl 14,277 VX4/90 & 25,185 Ventora).

Following a gap in availability, the VX4/90 was offered again after two seasons. Note the distinctive white cross grille and Rostyle wheels on this striking red example.

The uprated dashboard of the VX4/90, similar to the Ventora but with its own VX4/90 motif on the passenger side.

PERFORMANCE: 1600cc & VX4/90 **Top speed**: 90-100mph (145-160kph); **0-60mph (100kph)**: 19.3 & 12.4 sec; **average economy**: 18-22mpg (Ventora), 24-28mpg (Victor & VX4/90).
PRICE AT LAUNCH: £819 base Victor 1600, £1101 (Ventora), £1203 (VX4/90).
MEASUREMENTS: **length**: 14ft 8¼in (4.48m); **width**: 5ft 7in (1.7m); **height**: 4ft 7¼in (1.4m); **wheelbase**: 8ft 6in (2.59m); **weight**: 2388lb (1084kg); **wheels**: 13in; **turning circle**: 30ft 4in (9.2m); **fuel capacity**: 12 gallons (54 litres); **boot capacity**: 25.8ft^3.
TECHNICAL: **engine types**: 1599, 1975cc, four-cyl, petrol, 3294cc, six-cyl, petrol; **gearbox**: four-speed manual, two-speed Powerglide, three-speed Strasbourg automatic; **suspension**: independent wishbone, coils (front), live axle, coil (rear); **brakes**: disc (front) & drums (rear).
TRIM: Vynide, Ambla.
KEY OPTIONAL EXTRAS: automatic transmission, overdrive, radio, fog lamps, reversing lights, over-riders.

Victor, Ventora and VX4/90 FE

March 1972 saw the introduction of the so-called Transcontinental FEs, a fresh-looking Vauxhall based on the Opel Rekord floor-plan. These stylish cars certainly brought an updated 1970s look to Vauxhall with a new range of fresh colours. They came with two revised 'slant-four' engines of an enlarged capacity (1759cc and 2279cc), which were also carried over into some of the new HC range and the Bedford CF van. The press was eager to test them, with lots of reports from even the smaller-run magazines of the day. Like the Viva and Magnum HCs, the estate version had an attractive raked rear screen giving it a real sporty look, although at a slight cost to internal capacity (now 67ft^3).

Once again, the VX4/90 headed up the sporting side of the model, with the 3.3-litre straight-six Ventora playing the luxury card, including a limited edition all-black VIP model. The 3294cc was also available in an estate form, too, albeit badged as Victor until October 1973 when, finally, the Ventora badge was used and models also now received a black front grille. Again, these Victors sold well, and a 2300S special edition was also marketed (first seen at the October 1974 Earl's Court Motor Show) with black vinyl roof, bright mouldings and special trim and coachlines. DTV also marketed its Sportpart conversion from 1975, with bodywork, engine and exhaust changes totalling £340 extra.

The FEs went largely unchanged until early 1976, when they were quietly replaced on the price lists by the VX cars with the same bodyshell, but sold less well than the new Cavaliers that had just been launched.

The Victor FE saloon: this 1975 model has the later darkened front grille.

Victor FE estate in SL form: looking at the wheels this is the rarer 3.3-litre model.

An early bright orange Ventora FE saloon press car. Ventora estate versions came a little later.

A blackened grille and a red Griffin badge seen on this 1974 season Ventora FE.

Side profile of the mid-season VX4/90 FE in blue. Note the thin chrome strips just above the sill line and at the rear, too.

A 1975 orange VX4/90 now with chrome wheelarch surrounds but now no chrome sill strips!

The 3.3-litre Ventora was also dropped, and customers would have to wait over two years until the bigger Royale arrived if they wanted a six-cylinder ride. Over 44,000 were produced, and the Victor name had vanished forever after 19 years.

The VX4/90 FE was an interesting car. Unlike the FB, FC and FD cars. It joined the FE range from day one with extra instrumentation and sports image, plus overdrive between 1972-'73. The adverts stated "Because there's more to life than commuting, shopping and taking the kids to school." Production of the Victor and Ventora stopped in late 1975, and the VX4/90 disappeared from the price lists in March 1976, only to reappear in mid-1977 (see below).

Vauxhall VX 1800 and 2300 FE

These new VX models may have looked just like their Victor predecessors by way of a casual glance, but were effectively a brand new range that clumsily rivalled the (cheaper) new Mk1 Cavalier. Early 1976 launch prices were £2592 (VX 1800), £2709 (VX 2300) and later in 1976 £3688 (VX 2300 GLS). All-new trim was evident throughout, new colour range, new rear axle design, revised cylinder heads and new carburettors, a higher mesh front grille was fitted and the top line 2300 GLS (saloon only) looked a million dollars in Copperstone Starfire metallic paint with a vinyl roof and Deerskin upholstery, and its luxury was heavily leaned on by the advertising copywriters. The advert stating "A practical alternative to yoga lessons" was published

in June 1978, just as FE production was coming to a halt in Luton. Over and above the standard models, the much dearer GLS boasted wool-cloth headlining, more carpeted areas, better sound insulation, vinyl roof, front air dam spoiler, extra bright-work, rubber bumper inserts, Ventora-style four halogen headlamps and uprated wheel trims.

The estate VX 1800/2300 model cost around an extra £211, and its Ambla-only trim was replaced by velour in 1977. Thankfully touring mpg figures were higher – around 29mpg was now possible.

With the inception of the bigger Carlton and Royales, by October 1978 the FE had taken its final bow – except for the Hindustan Contessa models, which were still produced in India, and were 're-invented' from 1984 through a variety of face-lifts, until their demise in 2002.

VX 490 (phase 2) FE

After a 15-month production gap, the VX 490 (note its slightly different designation) appeared again in March 1977, following an unlikely rather early launch at the Malmo Motor Show in Sweden. The new car price lists in the weekly press reintroduced the VX 490 in late August 1977 at £4261, sitting between the VX 2300 at £3586 and VX 2300 GLS at £4564.

Hardly a rival to the new, home-grown and sturdy Volvos also on display there, the five-speed car used the dog-leg first gear Getrag gearbox rather than the Firenza ZF unit, and had twin carburettors. The more sporty-looking interior was completely different to the sister VX cars, use of the Magnum/Chevette bold plaid cloth seat-trim and door cards was evident, and the dash made use of a 'black crackle' plastic finish, instead of wood. Externally there were Rostyle wheels, more chrome and the deeper spoiler from the 2300 GLS model. Window surrounds (and centre panel on rear) were finished in satin black. Research for this book revealed no national press adverts for this phase II VX 490, with only a single sales catalogue, but it was included in the 1977 and 1978 all-model brochures. Just over 900 VX 490s were produced 1977-'78, mainly sold in

The short-lived five-speed phase 2 VX 490 of 1977/8 and its 'black crackle' instrument panel.

The bold plaid cloth seat and door trim of the VX 490; also standard fitting in the 2300HS Chevette and Magnum Sportshatch.

A VX 2300 GLS automatic was about as good as it got in the top line FE department. These FEs had full-depth chrome sill covers, plus extra bright-work but no headrests!

The same model from a front three-quarter angle, this one sporting the popular silver metallic finish, with vinyl roof fitted as standard, again on a top model. The deep front spoiler was also used in the later run-out VX 490.

the home market making this a very rarely seen car. Previous research in 1989 by the author revealed many pictures in the Vauxhall press office of a proposed 118mph VX 490 model with fuel-injection that sadly could not be used for a previous project.

FE media advertising slogans

The Transcontinentals
For people who want the usefulness of an estate with the styling of a car (estate)
Six 'extras'. No extra cost! It's a joy to drive
Gain all round with the DTV Victor (2300)
It's a joy to drive! (Ventora)
It's rather like having a built-in chauffeur (Ventora)
For the director who can't decide (Ventora estate)
Value has never been better. And never so luxurious (2300S)
The most beautiful thing about it is the people who buy it (VIP Ventora)
Meet the hot transcontinental (1972 VX4/90)
High-flier for the family! (VX4/90)
Because there's more to life than commuting, shopping and taking the kids to school (early VX4/90)
Five caravan races. Five Vauxhall victories (VX4/90)
For those who like to sit down and relax before they get home (VX 2300)
A guided tour around our estate (VX 2300 estate)
Take twice daily to relieve backache, fatigue and tension (VX 1800/2300)
A practical alternative to yoga lessons (VX 2300 GLS)

FE BODY TYPES: four-door saloon, five-door estate; **production run**: 1972-1978; **manufactured at**: Luton; **number produced**: 44,078 (Victor 1800/2300), 693 (3300 estate), 7291 (Ventora), 18,042 (1972-75 VX4/90), 25,815 (VX), 900 (VX 490 1977-78).

Country Life magazine carried this VX 2300 GLS advert claiming the GLS was a practical alternative to yoga lessons! Note sumptuous interior with rear armrest, all for £4792 in 1978.

Just ahead of the impending GLS launch, this period advert depicts a "relaxing" VX 2300 velour interior, yours for £2708 all-in, including a 12-month unlimited mileage guarantee.

PERFORMANCE: 0-60mph: 17.3/11.1 sec; **top speed**: 89/105mph (1800 & VX 490); **average economy**: 18-22mpg (3300 cars), 23-30mpg (1800 & 2300 cars).
PRICE AT LAUNCH: £1299 (2300SL Victor).
MEASUREMENTS: **length**: 14ft 11in (4.55m); **width**: 5ft 7in (1.7m); **height**: 4ft 6in (1.37m); **wheelbase**: 8ft 9in (2.66m); **weight**: 2445-2765lb (1109-1254kg); **wheels**: 13in (14in on 3300); **turning circle**: 35ft 10in (10.9m); **fuel capacity**: 14¼ gallons (65 litres), boot capacity 21ft^3.
TECHNICAL: **engine types**: 1759, 2279cc, four-cyl, petrol, 3294cc, six-cyl petrol; **gearbox**: four-speed manual, five-speed manual, three-speed automatic, Laycock overdrive (1972-73); **suspension**: independent wishbone, coils (front), live axle, coil (rear); **brakes**: disc (front) & drum (rear).
TRIM: Ambla, cloth, velour.
KEY OPTIONAL EXTRAS: Laycock overdrive on Victors 1972-73, tow bar, rear safety belts, hazard warning device, vinyl roof, reversing lights.

Small family cars: Viva HA, HB and HC including Firenza and Magnum

Viva HA

Affectionately nicknamed the 'Biscuit Tin,' the Viva HA was the first of three Vivas released between 1963 and 1979. Launched in September 1963 as "The 1-litre car with a millionaire ride," this was a small nimble saloon that quickly tackled the lucrative bottom end of the UK market. Vauxhall had not seen such an entry level car since 1936. The new Viva was available in various trim guises and always with the 1057cc four-cylinder petrol engine, and in two-door rear-wheel drive saloon format. All van versions were badged as Bedfords, production of which lasted for three years after the demise of the HC Viva, and an incredible 16 years after the original Viva HA saloon was discontinued.

Relying on valuable research and development performed by Opel, it was decided from early on that the amount of space required by passengers and their luggage was more important than how compact the overall dimensions of the car were. However, its size was indeed quite compact, the new vehicle being 18 inches shorter than the Victor FB with which it rubbed shoulders in the salerooms, yet it could still swallow nearly 11ft^3 of luggage in the boot. Vauxhall had carefully considered a rear-engined concept with front-wheel drive, but came to the conclusion early on in the design project that this would impair boot capacity if it was to include an estate version. Ironically, no HA estate ever existed (much to the delight of Ford, with its notchback Anglia 105E) except the Bedford Beagle outside conversion, based on the van covered later in this chapter.

A two-door only passenger body was chosen as they are always lighter, stiffer and cheaper to produce, and the very wide doors made the access to the rear compartment exceptionally easy. The front suspension was not coil as you might expect, but a transverse elliptic leaf spring (wheel-to-wheel) that also acted as a roll stabiliser. At the rear there was a live axle, with half-elliptic leaf springs on each side. The new engine weighed just 50lb heavier than the alloy unit used in a main rival, the Hillman Imp, much design work was performed to keep this 227lb cast iron unit as light as possible. Gears were selected by a short lever on the floor connected to a new four-speed plus reverse gearbox, using synchromesh in all its forward gears. It certainly was a very light gear change.

An early production Viva HA. Rear side windows could be opened via hinges.

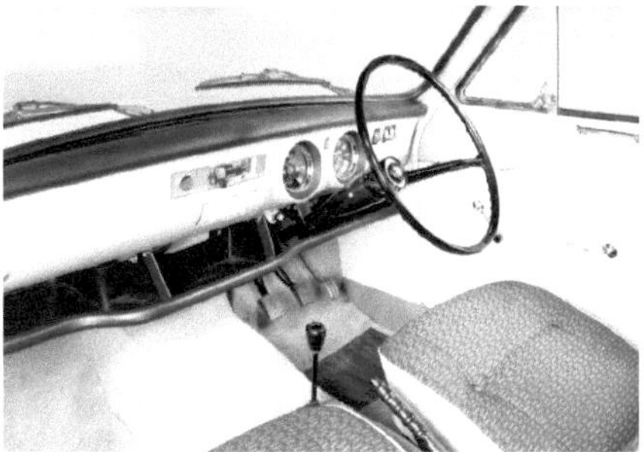

Although it looked spartan, cloth trim and carpets were fitted on this Viva HA deluxe from 1963.

A tidy-looking Viva HA SL, photographed in Bridgnorth, 2022.

A Viva HA SL with two-tone side flash and whitewall tyres.

Another Viva HA SL with chrome wheel embellishments.

Viva HA deluxe advert from 1965. "The Viva had the lightest steering effort of any car in its class ..."

Considerable work was performed to seal the body against rust after much criticism of the Victor F and PA cars.

In summer 1963, following the secret press gathering at the very plush Abernant Lake Hotel in secluded rural Llanwrtyd Wells in Powys, Wales, a very damp seven-day 800-mile model demonstration commenced with fully badged cars. The press was reporting favourably about the model's small dimensions, light controls and a delightful gear change. Initially a basic saloon and deluxe model were sold, the base model missing a passenger sunvisor, heater and screen-washer, and any aluminium trim along the body sides. Both models had opening front quarter-lights, rear side windows opened by 2½in on the deluxe model only, and decorative trim surrounding the front and rear windscreens. The trim was better on the deluxe, which featured carpets throughout, whereas the base model made do with moulded rubber floor mats. A padded cloth black material covered the fascia of the deluxe, and there were ashtrays and armrests in the rear. Six paint

The hot Viva HA 90 'red' engine.

colours were offered for the base model, and nine for the deluxe.

The various assembled press members drove these early prototypes in the gruelling Welsh hills for several days. *Motor* magazine reported in its 27th September 1963 issue: "It is a very roomy car in comparison with its main competitors, well insulated from road noise and with really lightweight controls." Several other magazines also reported on how light the car was to drive. "Taking into account the ease of seeing all four wing edges from the driving seat and the Viva's turning circle ... the car was both easy to handle and to park," stated *Practical Motorist* magazine in 1964. At the time of launch, Vauxhall stated its new car was best in its class when it came to power to weight ratio.

Within a year of launch, the door cards received two-tone colour treatment and the armrests were padded, and, to avoid excessive rotation of the steering wheel, the steering gear ratio was raised by 20 per cent. The previous wafer-thin seats were uprated giving better support whilst cornering, and under the bonnet modifications included thermostat setting improvements to reduce cold engine warm up time. The incredible 100,000 production milestone was achieved within 10 months of the launch.

Tuned examples soon followed; one such conversion performed by Bob Henderson of MPG&H of Hackbridge, Surrey. Its unusually named Fish Viva gave an extra 15mph top-end, and shaved a useful six seconds from the 0-60mph acceleration time by replacing the standard Solex carburettors with a revised unit that gave an extra 6hp. The cost was £30 fitted, and the loud roar from the new carburettor setup was a memorable eyebrow-raiser!

Another more comprehensively prepared conversion in 1964 was the LawrenceTune Viva GT for an all-in price of £789. It came with racing bucket seats, wooden-rimmed steering wheel, suspension and cylinder head modifications. It was good for 88mph and knocked five seconds off the 0-60mph time.

In summer of 1965, a Viva averaged 47.08mpg on the then 26-year-old Mobil Economy Run, using Mobil lubricants exclusively. The run, an annual event designed to provide real fuel efficiency numbers, took place on standard roads. To answer criticism, the foot pedals were moved an inch-and-a-half to the right.

The top SL (Super Luxury) model announced later in 1965 had a new polished aluminium front grille (with Vauxhall badge built in), bumper over-riders, wheel embellishments, coloured side flashes and better interior trim, with Ambla upholstery and a new-look matt silver finish facia with locking glovebox. Distinct black figures on matt silver dials (now showing up to 100mph) completed the look, and the horns were now twins. Revised rear identification included an SL badge on the right side of the boot lid and individual round lamps on the rear for turning, side and stopping. The Viva script was moved from the back to the leading edge of the front wings.

The Viva 90 model was the first factory Viva sold to get an upgraded engine (painted red), and was available on the deluxe (£606) or new SL platform (£648) from October 1965. Adverts stated: "Book your seats now for the most exciting 1-litre performance of the year ..." The original 44hp engine was increased in power to 54hp and had a higher compression ratio, whilst a Stromberg carburettor replaced the Solex. This resulted in a better top speed of 85mph and improved acceleration, reducing the 0-60mph time by three seconds. To allow for this extra power, the rear propshaft was also uprated. The HA continued until the introduction of the HB in October 1966.

HA van and Bedford Beagle

Ten months after the introduction of the HA saloon, the Bedford HA van made an appearance in the small commercial marketplace, and was soon popular with both large fleet corporate buyers and tradesmen. Two versions were available: the 6cwt (HAE) and 8cwt (HAV), the latter with heavier rear springs, a beefier rear axle and stronger wheels. These small commercials soon provided convenient load transportation via their twin opening rear door arrangement and 61ft^3 internal capacity in the back. Further room was found in the front as the passenger seat was optional. The roof line was 4in higher than the saloon, and a 2in deeper windscreen design was utilised. For a lot of extra storage, the factory offered a very limited number of high roof HA vans in the mid-1960s, with internal capacity now up to 91ft^3. As Viva car production moved forwards, the little HA van battled on in incredible fashion, utilising each of the later Viva engines until its demise in 1982, in the guise of the HA110 and HA130. Indeed, there was a record order taken in 1973, constituting 3200 Viva vans for the Royal Mail.

A pick-up design was considered in the early 1970s, and a few examples were built with a flip-down rear tailgate. Certainly a few of the factory-approved Walker-Bedford conversions still exist, and are sometimes seen at car shows. Larger customers included the gas, water and electricity boards, plus Royal Mail, Post Office Telephones, BEA and British Rail. A rather deluxe dark metallic blue version, the Double Plus, was marketed in 1973 with black front grille (this was later adopted on production vans) and pinstripes, and the optional extra fold-down seat in the back for occasional customers.

Within weeks of the van announcement came news of the Martin Walter conversion to a plusher, passenger-carrying Bedford Beagle, a kind of Talbot Matra Rancho of the 1960s. Designed for family holidays or weekend chores, the new "Designed to be a busy Beagle" was marketed by the Folkestone firm as an estate car, with emphasis on carrying capacity, visibility, performance and good looks. It sold for £624 and was trimmed to Martin Walter's coach-building standards, with fold-down rear seating and opening side windows. Like the vans, it was 5in shorter than the saloons, with a reduced rear overhang. Additionally, the Roma Dormobile was also produced by Martin Walter, and used a pop-up tailgate that revealed an opening storm-proof rear extension and traditional Dormobile raising roof section. A gas cooker, ample cupboards, foldaway table and wash basin

The Martin Walter-converted Bedford Beagle had sliding side windows and its own chrome 'Beagle' badge on the front wings.

A 1981 HA van. The gas board was amongst its loyal fleet buyers in its later days, despite the availability of the Chevanne and later Astravan.

A summer 1982-registered HA van in attractive metallic blue, on a recent Suffolk classic vehicle run.

were included for a small family of three, and when all popped away, yes, it would fit in a small garage. The Roma Dormobile was £1062 new in 1972, which was around the same price as the Vauxhall Viva HC deluxe estate at the time.

HA media advertising slogans

How do you go to the country in style, right warmly in a Viva deluxe
Best holiday package-deal yet
Five top features keep the Viva in the limelight
Eager Viva puts the sport in Transport (South Africa)
The GMH small car. Cuts the cost but not the pleasure
Go swiftly, safely Viva!
Is this the year you own a Viva
The 1-litre car with the millionaire ride
How do you go to the countryside in style? Right warmly (deluxe)
If you're looking for luxury in a car (SL)
Motoring is an all year holiday in the brilliant, carefree Viva
Park Tall (Roma Dormobile)
Stylish, practical and easy to drive (Bedford)
Roomiest light delivery van on the road (Bedford)
These trim, tough newcomers are with it – with everything! (Bedford)
Family runabout or busy workhorse (Beagle)
Designed to be a busy Beagle (Beagle)
Work hard and play hard (it's an obedient car!) (Beagle)
Don't poodle about, better buy Beagle (Beagle)

HA BODY TYPES: two-door saloon, van & converted vans: 1963-1966 (saloon), 1963-1982 (van); **manufactured at**: Ellesmere Port; **number produced**: 309,538, 11,794 (90 model)
PERFORMANCE: **top speed**: Viva 75mph (120kph,) Beagle/Roma 71mph (114kph); **0-60mph (100kph)**: 21 seconds; **average economy**: 35mpg.
PRICE AT LAUNCH: £527.
MEASUREMENTS: **length**: 12ft 11in (3.94m) saloon, 12ft 6in (3.81m) van; **width**: 4ft 11½in (1.51m); **height**: 4ft 5¼in (1.36m) & 4ft 11½in (1.51m) van; **weight**: 1603lb (728kg) & 1750lb (749kg) van; **wheelbase**: 7ft 7¾in (2.33m); **turning circle**: 27ft 4in (8.33m); **fuel capacity**: 7 gallons (32 litres); **wheel size**: 12in; **boot capacity**: 10¾ft^3, van/Beagle 61ft^3.
TECHNICAL: **engine types**: 1057cc, four-cyl petrol on cars plus 1159cc, 1256cc four-cyl petrol on later vans; **gearbox**: four-speed synchromesh, floor change; **suspension**: transverse leaf (front), live axle, leaf half-elliptic (rear); **brakes**: drum all round, front discs optional.
KEY OPTIONAL EXTRAS: sill tread plates, heater, screen-washer, passenger sunvisor (on base models), front disc brakes with vacuum assistance, choice of radio, fog lamps, aerial, temperature gauge, tow bar, seat covers, wing mirrors, anti-dazzle mirror, cigarette lighter, roof rack, seatbelts, wheel embellishments and reversing lamps (on all models), hi-top facility, seat kit and ladder rack (van).

Viva HB

Replacing the three-year-old Viva HA, the attractive HB series of cars made their debut in October 1966, initially available as just a two-door saloon, followed by a three-door estate in 1967 and four-door saloon version in 1968. Styling was the popular Coke-bottle variety, as seen in 1967 on the new FD Victor range. In a first for Vauxhall, there was front and rear coil spring suspension, and a bigger body - it was 7in longer and 3in wider than the HA - meant more room inside, easily carrying five occupants. Passengers enjoyed the comfort of more vinyl covering - gone were the days of large, plain, painted areas inside the passenger compartment. By enlarging the cylinder bores, engine displacement was up to 1159cc, again with four-cylinders in pushrod form, with bigger engine options for the HB to follow.

Once again, a higher performance 60hp 1159cc Viva 90 was available from the outset in deluxe and SL format, with lower axle ratio for improved acceleration (0-60mph in 15.2 seconds). It was also available later in estate form as the SL90.

Whilst a standard (HBS) base model was available to the fleet market (no sunvisor, lack of front opening quarter-lights and heater and windscreen washers were optional), the public had the choice between deluxe (HBD) and SL (HBH) trim from the outset. With enhanced trim and sculptured seating, the SL interior received a plastic wood-style cover on the facia and glovebox, and a useful tray was placed over the transmission tunnel.

The Viva HB in four-door form.

A carefully posed picture just 25 miles north of the Luton factory, with the help of the local constabulary. Note the pop-up police sign on the boot.

The fastback Viva HB estate displays bright red interior trim throughout.

SL models gained front discs over the base model's drums, and these were servo assisted. Identification was easy at the front, as SLs had a more upmarket front grille.

Specialist Jack Brabham-tuned Vivas were identified by distinctive wing and bonnet stripes, giving an additional 9hp with the 1159cc engine (now with Stromberg carburettors), and utilising front disc brakes. The cost was £598 in 1967, which sat nicely between the standard 998cc Mini Cooper at £512 and the Mini Cooper 1275S at £690.

The £68 option of the Borg Warner Type 35 gearbox was quietly added in February 1967, and the motoring press was quick to point out that such Vivas were amongst the slowest cars on the road so-equipped. It was available in deluxe or SL and 90 forms.

The (two-door only) estate car became part of the range in June 1967, an official

Another four-door HB with optional wing mirrors and driving lamps.

An early production Brabham Viva HB conversion.

Brabham advertising. The same dusty image was used in other media adverts, minus the Brabham artwork!

production line product – no more outside conversions, this was a fastback style, but could still swallow 53ft^3 of luggage with a high-lifted counterbalanced rear tailgate. It shared the same body length as the saloon, and an automatic option was offered from October 1967. The specific model designations were HBW (deluxe) and HBG (SL) estates.

"Smooth and quiet. Smooth and flexible," the adverts stated for the new Viva 1600. The optional 84hp Victor FD slant-four 1599cc engine was fitted to Vivas from June 1968, with stiffer suspension and low profile tyres, and 83mph now available in two-door, four-door and estate form. Deluxe OHC or SL OHC badges were fitted to the front wings and boot panels. The 1600 proved only slightly faster than the 90, but seemed to use almost as much petrol as the 2-litre GT. *Autocar* recorded an overall consumption of just 23mpg with its long-term 1600cc test car (albeit automatic) in 1970, whilst rival *Motor* obtained 28mpg overall with its manual Viva 90 over a 12,000 mile test in 1968.

The lusty FD engine-powered 2-litre Viva GT came in two varieties, both twin-Zenith carburettor. The first phase in March 1968

Ye Olde Vauxhall Inn and a brand new Viva GT. The pub still exists in Tonbridge, Kent.

Press day for the new Viva GT with all cars in the 'PXD F' series.

The more restrained-looking later Viva GT, now with body-coloured bonnet and Rostyle wheels.

had special wheels, black rear panel, matt black bonnet complete with scoops, wing stripes, four exhaust tail-pipes, chrome wheel trims, 10in front disc brakes and a general aggressive appearance. Inside was a multi instrumentation dashboard with 120mph speedometer, electric clock, oil temperature, rev counter, oil pressure, ammeter, water temperature gauges etc, with special bucket seats, all-black trim and a leather covered steering wheel. It was a creditable 112hp and featured special front and rear axles, plus clutch and Cresta-developed gearbox. This car looked and sounded fast, and other road users were made aware of the top specification by a Viva GT script on the rear wings, just in front of the rear lamp clusters and red GT badge on the black grille. *Car* magazine tested an early example: "At the moment £1022 is a bit much to be asking for a car which is excessively noisy, wrongly geared, has a poor driving position if you are at all big, and displays some tricky handling in tight situations ..." *Hot Car* described it as "a mixed up motor car."

Following the many negative comments in the motoring press, it was replaced by a more conservative version in October 1969 with toned-down looks: it now featured the more attractive Rostyle wheels, a body-coloured bonnet and a whole host of smaller improvements, including to the switch-gear. This was the quickest HB of all, with a top speed of a shade under 100mph and 0-60mph in just under 11 seconds. 4606 were produced in its two and a half year run. Towards the end of its production, *Motor* magazine commented in its GT brief road test "a promise fulfilled." Retrospectively, tuner Bill Blydenstein converted a GT, VLT513G, and *Car* magazine tested it in 1971, obtaining 108mph and 0-60mph in just 8.5 seconds. ..

"Look dad. Four-door!" was the advert title in September 1968 with the introduction of the four-door saloon model which instantly brought in higher sales. It looked so much better than the rival Mk1 Escort four-door, which seemed to be more of an afterthought. Complete doors were imported from Australia from the GM Holden plant, and the extra price of the deluxe was £45 over the two-door version. The new front doors were now narrower, but access to both front and rear compartments was still very reasonable for such a small car. At the same time the whole range had an energy absorbing steering column fitted, two-speed blower fan and improved panel layout. Relocation of important switchgear from under the dashboard to under the speedometer occurred, some of which was nearly impossible to use when the safety belts were in use. There were also revised door trims and window winders, and the SL model was available with a vinyl roof. There were various other modifications made before the end of production, particularly to alternator specification, and production had ceased by the summer factory closure in August 1970.

A Viva HB Prince luxury conversion was offered by Crayford Conversions, but suffered from poor sales. However, its HB convertible two-door SL was more successful, marketed through Wallace Arnold of Leeds. Very few survive.

The HB was also sold and built overseas as Chevrolet/Oldsmobile Envoy Epic in the USA, in South Africa, in Australia as the Holden Torana, and from CKD kits imported to New Zealand from the UK. No vans were produced on the HB platform, but estate cars with no rear seats were sold in New Zealand. The sister HA van continued as before, with various updates to bring it into line with contemporary vehicles.

HB media advertising slogans
... revel in that fast-off feeling (four-door)
You're fast in, fast off. With power to make the going good (four-door)
Vauxhall does it with style. She looks so slim (estate)
Look dad. Four-door (four-door)
For all those that thought their sports car days were over (GT)
Good news. Travels fast. Viva 1600 joins the breed
Brabham breathed on it. One of the ten called Viva (Brabham)
And you feel sportissimo (estate)
Flaunting a fastback. One of ten called Viva (estate)
Sensation! Viva goes topless! (convertible conversion)

HB BODY TYPES: two-door & four-door saloon, three-door estate: 1966-1970; **manufactured at**: Ellesmere Port; **number produced**: 566,391, (78,296 estates).
PERFORMANCE: **Base model top speed**: 80mph (128kph); **0-60mph (100kph)**: 19.5 sec; **average economy**: 25mpg (GT & 90), 28-30mpg (rest).
PRICE AT LAUNCH: £579 (base model).
MEASUREMENTS: **length**: 13ft 5½in (4.1m); **width**: 5ft 2¾in (1.58m); **height**: 4ft 6¾in (1.39m), wheelbase 7ft 11¾in (2.43m), weight (base model): 1725lb (782kg); **wheels**: 12in (& 13in GT); **turning circle**: 28ft (8.53m); **fuel capacity**: 8 gallons (36.4 litres), from 1968 12 gallons (54.6 litres); **boot capacity**: 16ft^3.
TECHNICAL: **engine types**: 1159cc, 1599cc, 1975cc (four-cyl, petrol); **suspension**: coil front and rear, live rear axle; **gearbox**: four-speed manual, Borg Warner automatic; **brakes**: drum all round, disc on front on larger-engined models.
TRIM: Vynide.
KEY OPTIONAL EXTRAS: automatic transmission, wing mirrors, heated rear window, alternator, radio (plus portable type), cigarette lighter, temperature gauge, reversing lights, fog lamps, locking fuel cap, over-riders, wheel trims, tow bar, front disc brakes.

Viva HC

Four years after the new HB Viva had been launched, the Viva HC was to take over, a new curvy model that was to stay around in various guises for nine years, eventually giving way to the Astra Mk1. Available from the outset as a two-door and four-door saloon, plus fastback three-door estate, the model was noticeably 2in wider but around the same length and height as its predecessor. To the modern eye, the tracking looks very narrow, with enormous wheelarches containing the skinny 4in rimmed, 13in wheels and 155 profile tyres, but in its day it was ultra modern. "The car we beat around ... to beat any car around" stated the adverts at launch, following its extensive design and test programme partly at the new Millbrook GM testing facility. This was to be the last Vauxhall passenger car wholly designed in the UK.

Mechanically, the HC was essentially unchanged from the HB cars save for a slightly uprated 1159cc engine (from 47hp to 50hp) – the optional 1599cc engine stayed as before, but hosted an all-new body welded to a modified version of the HB platform. The wheels were now 13in, and the final drive ratio was changed to compensate for this. There were numerous detail improvements,

The new Viva HC two-door saloon, the third and largest Viva.

A Viva HC two-door saloon under heavy test; a left-hand drive factory registered example, possibly at the company's Chaul End testing facility.

An early dashboard of a Viva automatic with fitted radio.

too, including new door locks that evolved in conjunction with AC Delco. Production started just after the summer break in September 1970.

Following a secret press launch in Divonne, France, 250 miles south east of Paris, again the French were the first to see the new model publicly at the Paris Motor Show from October 1st, 1970 – a couple of weeks ahead of the

This elevation shot displays the attractive V-shaped bonnet creases very well on the HC estate.

Earl's Court London Motor Show, although the new cars were tucked away in the background, largely unnoticed. In London, several new Vivas were shown alongside the partitioned-off and stunning SRV concept car, which drew the crowds. The Coke-bottle look had given away to horizontal lines, thus the kick-up style line above the rear wheels had gone. The new range included a Standard (two-door only) model, a deluxe and a Super; the latter had extra bright-work and centre console, lockable glovebox, moulded fitted carpets, extra sound insulation and a boot light. It also had the uprated 90 engine fitted (no longer painted red and optional on deluxe), and servo assisted disc brakes. Boot space was a creditable 20/62ft^3 for the saloon/estate.

In the early 1970s conversions came from Blydenstein Racing via its workshop in Shepreth. Good for an extra 10mph top speed, these models sported a rear boot badge and received a fully modified cylinder head and downdraft Weber carburettor kit.

The first major production change occurred in September of 1971, with the upgrading of the 1159cc engine to 1256cc by increasing the piston bore diameter by 2mm. More effective air vents were also fitted. Within a few weeks, just after the London Motor Show, the optional 1599cc engine was dropped, and for the new model year, the slant-four 1800 and 2300-engined Viva was announced at the Geneva Motor Show in Switzerland, not far from the HC's launch nearly two years before. In the interim, the Viva Gold Riband became one of the first

A 1974 Viva HC two-door with matching sky blue-coloured trim.

limited edition models Vauxhall had ever produced. The 1256cc was fitted with Rostyle wheels and radial tyres, very early nylon-type cloth trim, heated rear window, front power disc brakes, hazard flashers, reversing lights, wall-to-wall carpets and a cigar lighter, and was described as "a new look in luxury." It came in a choice of three colours for paint and interior trim. Soon after came a second similarly specified special, the Viva X14, of which 6000 were built in 1256cc manual and 1759cc automatic format.

The new 1759cc slant-four engine, borrowed from the FE range, really transformed the HCs in the spring of 1972. To the slight detriment of fuel bills, performance was better, and cars came with uprated suspension, drivetrain, gearbox and tyres. The 2300 was to follow by summer 1972, and the best specification Viva was a 2300 SL estate capable of 100mph (often dubbed 'the poor man's Scimitar GTE,' the Reliant offering similar performance but at nearly twice the price). The key difference inside: the largest-engined Viva favoured the new seven-dial dashboard layout seen on the Firenza, whilst the 1800 unit retained the earlier oblong speedometer layout. The short-lived 2300 version was discontinued with the arrival of the Magnum in September 1973.

From around March 1973 (in UK 'L' registration time), the front wings were altered. Gone were the pointy top versions in favour of a more flat-top appearance along their length, which in the author's opinion suited the flowing lines of the new silver HP Firenza so much more.

The £1073 Viva DS was marketed from mid-1974. Previously fleet sales provided larger driving school companies, but now Vauxhall was targeting the one-man-band outfits with the DS in conjunction with the Motor Schools Association. The £1557 Viva S offered extra luxury to the 1256cc range, such as chrome rear arch stone guards, special Green or Blue Starfire paintwork, vinyl roof, radio cassette, plush blue or black cloth reclining seats, special wheels and an 'S' badge motif on the boot-lid.

In October 1975, nylon upholstery was fitted into the mainstream SL models, and the 1256cc range was enlarged to include an 'E' – "Economy with a capital E" – version based on the fastback coupé, using the same shell as the Firenza/Magnum coupé. This was a "Hurry! Limited production only" model selling for £1399, some £180 less than the base two-door saloon of the time. In three colours, white plus blue and gold metallics, it came with reclining front seats, 'loop-pile' carpeting throughout, parcel shelf, glovebox and flick-on two-speed wipers. Unlike the rival Ford Escort

Reclining seats in a 1974 Viva interior.

The run-out 1978 1800 GLS Viva by now had the seven-dial dashboard, and was basically a Magnum in all but name. Later cars had the chrome stone guards ahead of the rear wheels, with velour seats. Four-door only on the 1800 GLS. The Viva 2300 was dropped when the Magnum was made available in 1973, but the 1800 Viva remained, which made for a confusing line-up of cars.

In 1976 those unsold Firenza/Magnum coupé shells were put to good use ... Enter the Viva E, the cheapest Viva in the range.

A Viva 1300L estate in the late 1970s.

Mk2 Popular, it had chrome bumpers and double coach-lines. Six months later came a similarly specified saloon E in both two- and four-door body at £1577 and £1646.

In 1977 there was a general refresh of appearance across the evergreen Viva range, as production had topped just 34,000 in 1976, compared to 72,000 two years before. "Introducing the most handsome Viva yet," the new 1300 GLS four-door model now had more luxury; velour trim, padded rear seat, fully trimmed doors, rear grab handles, inertia reel safety belts, pile carpeting, many electrical upgrades, and the seven-dial instrumentation from the Magnum. The Rostyle wheels complemented the extra chrome bright-work, rubber bumper inserts and fuel filler cap. Up front were the twin headlamps borrowed from the Magnum.

At the end of Viva's lifespan, the range was the E (saloon two- and four-door), the 1300L (two- and four-door plus estate), and 1300/1800 GLS (four-door only). In 1979 production ceased, making way for the new Vauxhall Astra, after over 640,000 cars had been produced, totalling an overall 16-year Viva production of around 1.5 million units. There was no commercial van version of the HC, although a Grumett was produced for the Uruguay market. The Viva name was revived by Vauxhall on a 2015 model.

Firenza and Magnum HC

Essentially, the Firenza started off as a sporting version of the Viva, available as an attractive coupé version in original 1159cc, and bigger 1599cc/1975cc FD-engined versions. The model enjoyed the same

A very early production Firenza. These cars did not fare well in Canada, with reliability issues from the outset.

Another early production Firenza. In the UK at least, Firenzas were all sold as coupés.

engine upgrades as its cheaper HC sister cars, namely the adoption of the 1256cc, then 1759cc and 2279cc units. Initially, all early variants received the very dull Viva strip speedometer and single headlamps, and the smaller-engined cars sold in low numbers; the bigger-engined cars (and the unusual 1256 SL) soon got a twin dial dash, then the exciting seven-dial dash was fitted in 2279cc cars, as later seen in the HP and Magnums. The Firenza name was used overseas for HC saloon cars, too. In Canada it was the last Vauxhall sold, due to several issues where an action group was formed against the company claiming unreliability and poor residual value. Vauxhall stopped exporting to Canada after 1972, having spent much research and development budget on getting the 2.3-litre engine ready for that market's tight emission regulations.

A larger-engined 1971 Firenza (see grille badge, either 1600 or 2000). Note Rostyle wheels. When the slant-four engines were fitted from 1972, the front grilles went black.

The top model was the Firenza sport SL with twin carburettors and flashy graphics, and yes, it was available as a Blydenstein-tuned conversion. Topping the Firenza SSL – which in itself was £100 dearer than the 2300 SL – was the maverick in the stable, the High-Performance Firenza, surely the Lotus Carlton of the mid-1970s. This was announced at the London Motor Show in October 1973, the HC range seemingly

Now with slant-four 2300 power, a 1973 sport SL Firenza attends a rally; the works Bedford CF rally support unit is parked behind.

The High Performance Firenza – note this model's black window surrounds.

Nose cone of the HP Firenza, and its own unique front wings.

One of the early production HP Firenzas, seen on press driving day.

Silver Bullet HC concept car photographed by the author in 1990.

undergoing a metamorphosis. It featured a very distinctive fibre-glass 'droop-snoot' front end, the result of a design overseen by Wayne Cherry, and was the first of several Vauxhalls to have this feature. The nose cone reduced the Cd drag factor from 0.484 to 0.404, with the boot spoiler getting the figure down further to an impressive 0.35Cd. The press was wild about the new car. *Motor* magazine, for example, posed one on the front cover of its 1973 show issue with a full-colour editorial inside. Whilst the story read well, entitled "No freak, no fills – the new Firenza," and quoted accurate performance figures. Sadly, the show guide section of the magazine quoted the new model as capable of only 97mph (156kph) with an unflattering 0-60mph of just 10.8 seconds, which was, of course, way off the mark. An exciting demonstration was organised by Vauxhall in May 1974, where 16 examples raced around the Thruxton race circuit. Also in attendance to tease the

The Magnum 1800 four-door. Note chrome wheel rims now fitted to these HCs.

The seven-dial dash was first fitted to 2300cc cars; later the 1800s, too.

Rear aspect of the Magnum 2300 coupé; another use for those unused Firenza shells! The model did not sell for long.

crowds was racing driver Gerry Marshall in the 500hp racing Repco Ventora V8.

Although it was hoped to sell 1000 per annum (with all examples built at the Ellesmere Port facility), just 204 were sold in the UK between May 1974 and June 1975 (at £2625), with a few extra development models built along the way and some export in both right- and left-hand drive cars. The 131hp car featured twin Zenith Stromberg carburettors, ZF five-speed gearbox, Bertone-styled Avon Safety wheels, a unique light grey cloth interior trim and came in Silver Starfire with contrasting black window surrounds. Over 120mph was possible, with an optimistic 0-60mph time of just 7.5 seconds, which some road testers actually achieved, rinsing rivals such as the Escort RS1600 and beating it to 100mph by around 6 seconds. The car was well received by the motoring hacks, but the difficult gear change was a common criticism. Known for preparing and maintaining rally cars, Perth Motors had marketed its own uprated HP Firenza R, and had secured the last 50 HP Firenzas in September 1975, which were extensively checked by their mechanics, including 50-mile road tests, then resold. They

Seen here in 1989, the HC Sportshatch was available in Bergundy with red style lines. There is still an enthusiastic following for these rare models.

A tidy Sportshatch interior, seen in 2022, shows the use of Bold Plaid trim on the door cards and seats. (Courtesy Tom Miller, Droop Snoot Group)

Bright yellow was a 1970s colour option! A very late Magnum four-door with vinyl roof.

in turn could have had the 'R' specification added at this late stage. Rumours of a top speed of 140mph were abound ...

The earlier, staid Firenza range was fairly short-lived, lasting until October 1973 when effectively it was replaced by the wider, smarter-looking Magnum range, and just the HP Firenza wore that badge. "Perhaps the only exciting luxury car at its price," was an advertising line that Vauxhall commonly used for the new Magnum, although another rarely seen advert compared the new model to the Porsche 911S Targa and Ferrari Dino 246 GT, where it could out-accelerate both in top gear between 30 and 50mph. Indeed when *Popular Motoring* magazine tested it in its February 1974 issue, a 0-60mph of just 9.4 seconds was recorded, with 104mph top speed.

The Magnum came in two-door and four-door saloons, a three-door estate and the same coupé body as the Firenza. The model was an attractive twin headlamp car with excellent interior appointments, such as seven-dial dash on the 2300 types and Rostyle road wheels, and was generally very well received by the press. It was fitted with top Viva's brakes and suspension, and was popular in motorsport in the 1970s. It was identifiable from the distant rear via a strip between the rear lights painted black with a red griffin motif in the centre, whereas the Firenza utilised body colour. Similarly, the front grille had a black background and advertised engine capacity on a small badge to the right. The 1800 had to wait until autumn 1975 for the seven-dial dash, and was then brought into line with its upmarket stable-mate with bigger tyres, better soundproofing and chrome trim – only their engines were now different. October 1975 saw deletion of the short-lived coupé (and the limited run Viva E coupé used any surplus bodyshells), and the 1800 went to single carburation. Blydenstein once again breathed on the car with several conversions available, including the Bentley Bros' Bee Bee and the GN Wasp-tuned versions in 1974.

Silver Bullet was an attractive one-off 2.3-litre estate version, built in 1974 and registered GNK31N. Since leaving Vauxhall it has been in enthusiasts' hands for many years. It had all the bells and whistles, including a very attractive nose cone similar to the HP Firenza's, but with very distinctive wider headlamp units and a fully trimmed interior. Following this was the 1976 Magnum Sportshatch: a very low production (197 made) estate car based on the 2300 Magnum platform and droop-snoot front end of the recently deleted HP Firenza, with the Avon Safety wheels, effectively using up surplus parts. It came in one colour – maroon with wide red striping – and featured a red bold plaid cloth interior. The engine was a less tuned version of the HP. Unlike the HP Firenza, the Sportshatch was not advertised in the national press, making it quite an unknown and sought-after Vauxhall.

There were no Magnums manufactured between May and October 1976. The last were registered in early 1978, just before the demise of the VX series, leaving the Vauxhall model range making room for the new Carltons and Royales, although the Viva continued until 1979. The existing Cavalier coupé and Sportshatch headed up the sports car market for Vauxhall. The last of the Magnums appeared on price lists, and the most expensive was still the 2300 estate at £3496, plus £269 with automatic transmission. Specialist manufacturer Panther had also based its fabulous Lima on the Magnum mechanicals at this time.

HC media advertising slogans

The car we beat around ... to beat any car around
The car that doesn't change for the sake of change
It went through a lot to give you a lot
Join Vauxhall in the fight against ugliness. And inflation (1800)
It's a joy to drive! (2300)
More action for your money (2300)
Proven reliability at a practical price (E)
A complete car at a popular price (E coupé)
The fantastic new Firenza sport SL (Firenza sport)
The super, sporting world of Firenza (Firenza sport SL)
0-60mph 7.5 seconds, 120mph, 40mpg (HP Firenza)
They've done much more. Dared hope (HP Firenza)
Vauxhall's 120+mph pace-maker (HP Firenza)
Leaves others fumbling in its wake (HP Firenza)
Perhaps the only exciting luxury car at its price (Magnum)
Which is fastest? (Porsche, Magnum, Ferrari) (Magnum)

HC BODY TYPES: two- & four-door saloon, three-door coupé, three-door estate: 1970-1979 (Viva), 1971-1973 (Firenza), 1973-1978 (Magnum); **manufactured at**: Luton & Ellesmere Port; **number produced**: 640,863 (Viva), 18,352 (Firenza), 20,300 (Magnum).
PERFORMANCE: **top speed**: 80mph (128kph); **0-60mph (100kph)**: 21 seconds (both 1159cc); **average economy**: 24mpg (1800/2300), 33mpg (rest).
PRICE AT LAUNCH: £783 (standard Viva), £2625 (HP Firenza).
MEASUREMENTS: **length**: 13ft 6in (4.11m); **width**: 5ft 4¾in (1.64m); **height**: 4ft 7in (1.4m); **wheelbase**: 8ft 1in (2.46m); **weight**: 1790lb-2374lb (812-1076kg); **wheels**: 13in; **turning circle**: 32ft 10in (10m); **fuel capacity**: 12 gallons (54 litres); **boot capacity**: 20ft^3.
TECHNICAL: **engine types**: 1159cc, 1256cc, 1599cc, 1759cc, 2279cc, all four-cyl, petrol; **gearbox**: four-speed manual, three-speed automatic; **suspension**: independent double wishbone, coil (front), live axle, coil (rear); **brakes**: drum all round, disc on front on larger-engined models.
TRIM: Vynide, Ambla, nylon, velour.
KEY OPTIONAL EXTRAS: performance 90 engine, automatic transmission, servo front disc brakes, heated rear window, reclining seats, vinyl roof on saloons, uprated radial tyres.

1960s opulence: PB and PC Cresta, Velox and Viscount

PB Cresta and Velox

The London Motor Show 1962 was used as the first platform for displaying the new lighter flagship Vauxhall cars, the PB Velox and Crestas, using completely different styling to the previous American influenced design. These cars were nearly 2in wider and 3in longer than their predecessors and sat commendably half an inch lower. Styled by David Jones, Vauxhall's chief styling engineer, they did indeed look familiar; the doors were identical to the second generation Victor FB first seen the year before, just as the 1948 L-Type had borrowed the prewar Ten's doors. BLMC copied this trick in 1968 with the new Austin Maxi hatchback, which inherited its doors from the BLMC Austin/Morris 1800 and derivatives, both these running concurrently for six years.

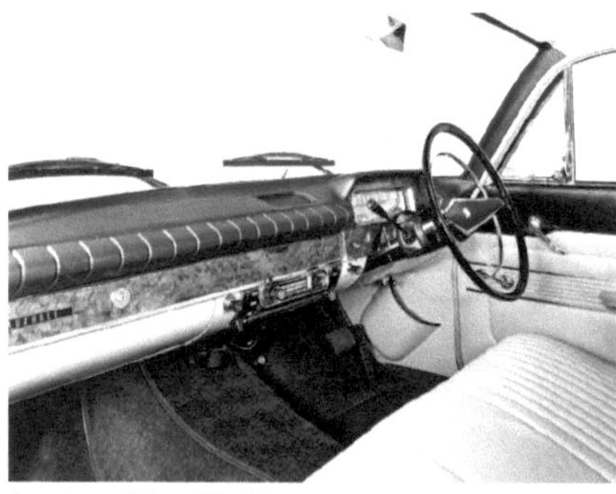

Interior of the PB. Note the deep map pocket on the driver's kick panel and lockable glovebox.

The wide radiator grille was slightly pointed in the middle, inspired by the old Prince Henry Vauxhall. Body lines were now straight rather than curved, and the rear window arched further round the side, resulting in a slimmer 'C' pillar. The Cresta received a full length chrome strip just under the window line, polished wheel trims and white side-wall

An early Velox PB in left-hand drive form.

A later Cresta PB in two-tone form.

tyres. With the improved dimensions, there was simply much more room inside, with an impressive six extra inches of legroom. Under a wide cowl in front of the driver sat the instrument panel, which tilted slightly upwards, housing the (colour variable-to-speed again) strip speedometer and a whole host of other instruments. Walnut veneer was used for this and the full width dashboard. The parking brake was now relocated to a position beside the seat cushion for easier operation. Interior trim was available in blue, green, grey or red, the Cresta with the option of two-tone leather A quality featured was the inclusion of handy leather straps above each rear to door assist passengers in getting out.

Rear aspect of a Swiss-registered Cresta PB. Note twin exhaust outlets.

An early PB Velox in single-tone colour. No whitewall tyres for the cheaper Velox.

Engines and gearboxes (including existing overdrive and the Hydra-Matic automatic) were directly brought over from the previous PAs, and indeed lasted until the end of the second year PB production in 1964. Through the three-speed manual gearbox, the near 100mph top speed and 0-60mph acceleration times were improved over the previous cars to around 14 seconds. Servo-assisted Lockheed disc brakes up front and drums at the rear were standard on both models apart from some export markets that got drums all round. Gone were the US-influenced tail fins, wrap-round front/rear screens and ornate chrome trim of the PA model, in favour of a more conservative, clean-cut look. Considerable thought went into minimising corrosion by removing the under-body nooks and crannies

A later Cresta PB in London around 1965, fitted with optional driving lights. Note the revised grille.

seen on earlier cars. Body sills were ventilated so any moisture could evaporate and disperse.

Extra features used on the Cresta over and above the Velox (some being optional) included: sound insulation under the bonnet, an electric clock and screen washers, automatic reversing lights, fog and spot lamps, switches on all door frames for the roof lamp, fold-up armrest on bench front seat model, fresh air heater/screen demister (optional on the Velox) and lockable fascia cubby hole.

By spring 1963, both models received large metal badging on the front wings just above the waistline behind the axle line.

Several cars had been road tested by the UK press within a few months, *Popular Motoring* magazine in its August 1963 issue reporting: "You really can't throw this car around corners with complete abandon; if you do it rolls quite heavily and is inclined to dislodge the passengers. But it's far from being a competition carriage, so that's a small price to pay for the remarkable degree of comfort that one otherwise enjoys. It's a long distance, long legged car that doesn't tire you out. Yet it corners safely driven normally, needing only a little caution on wet and slippery bends at speed." It recorded a 93mph top speed, 0-60mph in 14.9 seconds and overall 18.9mpg overall on its three-speed manual test Cresta 760GMJ.

In October 1964, modifications were made across the range, and a more powerful 3.3-litre 128hp six-cylinder engine replaced the earlier units, raising overall power by 21 per cent. Top speed was now 100mph and 0-60mph was attained in 11.6 seconds, a gain of about 2½ seconds. The *Motor* magazine road test title cried "Ton up automatic ..." in the August 28th 1965 issue, published just a few weeks before the inception of the PC cars.

At this time, 'four-on-the-floor' manual transmission was a useful option, and Hydra-Matic transmission soon made way to flick on/flick off Powerglide two-speed automatic. Only the Cresta could be ordered with bench front seats, with or without reclining seat backs. All models now had variable speed wipers. Such revised models were identified by the new anodised aluminium grille, twin exhaust tail pipes, bright metal strips (lower down for the Cresta) along the body sides and on the bonnet. The Cresta also received reversing lights fitted within the tail light cluster. Magic Mirror acrylic paint was now available with ten new colours and two-tone treatment available for the Cresta.

Velox and Cresta PB estate

Back in 1773, the foundation of Folkestone converter Martin Walter was a family firm of horse saddlers and harness makers in Southgate, London. Its activities were extended to horse-drawn carriages and then vehicles by the turn of the 20th century. Decades later it was converting vans such as the Bedford CA into Dormobile caravanettes and minibuses, and cars into estate versions such as the Cresta and Velox E-series. Unlike earlier outsourced conversions, the PB Cresta and Velox estates were now directly advertised in the national press by Vauxhall itself, which indeed used its logo on the estate car brochures.

The cavernous 67ft^3 load-space was "inside the handsomest body of them all ..." as the 1964 copywriters boasted. The cars were available at £1203 (Velox) and £1305 (Cresta). As before, four-leaf springs were used instead of three to carry extra loads. During conversion, the whole of the rear of the saloon was removed (including its rear side doors), replaced by glass-fibre panels for the roof, tailgate and both rear wings, which also incorporated the recesses for the lamp units. The saloon rear side doors were not used; FB Victor estate units were fitted instead to accommodate the slightly different style line. Martin Walter also converted the little Bedford HA van into the Bedford Beagle, amongst work with other manufacturers, too. There was a brand new Martin Walter PB estate conversion on display at the 1963 London Motor Show in the coachwork section.

A Cresta estate conversion by Martin Walter of Folkestone. The whitewall tyres and two-tone paint treatment are retained.

Harold Radford PB Cresta conversion

Also displayed at the coachwork section of the Earl's Court Motor Show in 1963 was the luxurious Harold Radford saloon conversion, applied to the PB Cresta.

Following the firm's upmarket Mini conversion, popular with film and rock stars alike, the Radford Cresta featured twin headlamps, front and rear over-riders, built-in fog lamps and a radically new front grille. Inside, the armrests, seats and a cubby hole were all trimmed in expensive hide. Folding tables were built into the backs of the front seats, which in turn reclined and were height adjustable. Extra instrumentation was fitted within the modified fascia panel, and a glass division was offered to divide the chauffeur and his rear seat occupants, who had their own reading lamps! It was easily identified by from the rear thanks to a ribbed section between the rear lamp clusters, complete with 'V' insignia. Think of this as a forerunner to the PC Viscount, although it did cost £1524, and an optional sunroof was extra cash on top!

PB media advertising slogans

Learn what it means to have 113 brake horsepower right where you need it (Cresta)
Simply great (Velox)
Visiting Britain? It's easy to own one of these fine Vauxhalls
This is the rugged, practical robust, sensible new Velox
The look of quality and bigness where it counts (Velox)
It's big, it's beautiful, it's every inch a winner! (Velox)
The new Velox takes it easy at 85mph (Velox)
Opulence for less than £850 that's the Velox
The admirable Vauxhall Velox
When you test drive the new Velox sit in the back
The looks will win your heart at once
Meet the newest estate car. Vauxhall's immaculate Cresta (estate)
Spacious comfort, superb six-cylinder performance (estate)

PB BODY TYPES: four-door saloon, five-door estate: 1962-1965; **manufactured at**: Luton; **number produced**: 87,047.
PERFORMANCE: **top speed**: 92-100mph (148-160kph); **0-60mph (100kph)**: 14 & 11.4 sec (2.6 & 3.3-litre compared); **average economy**: 19-24mpg.
PRICE AT LAUNCH: £936 (Velox), £1046 (Cresta).
MEASUREMENTS: **length**: 15ft 2in (4.62m); **width**: 5ft 10¾in (1.8m); **height**: 4ft 10in (1.47m); **wheelbase**: 8ft 11¾in (2.74m), weight 2.6 & 3.3-litre: 2744lb (1245kg) & 3080lb (1397kg); **wheels**: 14in; **turning circle**: 35ft (10.7m); **fuel capacity**: 10¾ gallons (48 litres); **boot capacity**: 21½ft^3 (saloon), 67ft^3 (estate).
TECHNICAL: **engine types**: 2651, 3293cc (both six-cyl, petrol); **suspension**: independent coil spring & transverse wishbones (front), live axle with semi-elliptic leaf springs (rear); **gearbox**: two-speed Hydra-Matic, three-speed auto, three-speed manual, optional overdrive; **brakes**: disc (front), drums (rear).
TRIM: Vynide seats (Velox), leather or nylon suede (Cresta).
KEY OPTIONAL EXTRAS: Hydra-Matic transmission, heater (£15 on Velox), radio, fog lights, reversing lights.

PC Cresta

After 17 years the familiar Velox name was finally dropped from the Luton range with the discontinuation of the PB. In October 1965, press details were released along with the new PC range debut at the UK Motor Show at Earl's Court, London, where a white Cresta took centre rotating display on the company stand. This new car was to compete with the Zephyr Zodiacs range from Ford and big BMC sixes from BLMC, namely the Wolseley and Vanden Plas cars. Rootes continued with its top-end Humbers, and direct comparisons were also made with prestige Mercedes-Benz and big Citroens.

This bold new Vauxhall, once again, was much longer – by nearly 6in – and although overall width was narrower by a cat's whisker, overall interior width was improved by 4½in at shoulder height with the new 'space-curve' Coke-bottle styling, as also soon seen on the sister FD series, albeit less angular. The new curved door glass design was carried over from the Victor FC. These cavernous cars often had trouble fitting into modestly sized domestic UK garages; by way of example, the modern day Tesla Model 3 is a similar width, but 2in shorter than the PC. As an advantage, it had an impressive 30ft^3 boot capacity – almost double that of its predecessor. The fuel tank was increased by 50 per cent, too, now at 15 gallons, allowing the PC extra range. It could still seat six in comfort when fitted with the standard front bench seat. The trademark GM longer tail and up-swept rear design was evident on the new models.

The engine remained the ex-Chevrolet 3294cc inherited from the PB, but in revised form, and now 12hp more powerful, giving rise to a rapid (for the period) 0-60mph acceleration time of just over 11 seconds, and a top speed of 104.6mph, as attained by *Practical Motorist* magazine in 1966. This was Lotus Cortina and Mini Cooper S territory, but from a large sedate-looking luxury saloon, and not forgetting the estate ...

There was a choice of four transmission types at launch: GM Powerglide (automatic), three-speed synchromesh with or without Laycock overdrive option, or four-speed synchromesh (manuals). All brakes had automatic adjustment with discs up front and drums at rear. Filling the larger fuel tank was now quicker thanks to improved non-spilling breather pipes, and the filler cap was concealed. Front independent coil spring suspension was again used, with rear semi-elliptic suspension variable.

This was the first Cresta to be fitted with fresh air ducts, aimed at giving cool air at face level, although when driving at the recommended ten-to-two position a draught went up the driver's sleeve! The heating system was improved with a quicker warm-up time, and there were new upholstery and trim materials used, including the option of leather on the deluxe (£14 15s) which could also be ordered with individual (then leather-only) front seats. The column gear change remained, except when ordered with the four-speed manual gearbox. Genuine burr walnut veneer

An early production police specification Cresta PC on M1 motorway traffic duties pulls over a Bedford TK. This Cresta has a solitary driving light fitted – still a legal fitment at the time – and rarer base model single headlamps.

was polished to a high gloss for the full width dashboard, and there was genuinely thick door-to-door carpeting. One press criticism was that of poor oddments storage, with only a non-locking glovebox on the dashboard, and some 'non-sag' map pockets in the front doors on the standard Cresta. However, the deluxe with individual front seating was equipped with extra storage on the rear of the front seats.

Up front there were differences between the entry model Cresta (PCS) and more upmarket Cresta deluxe (PCD) that weighed in 34lb heavier. The most obvious was the adoption of twin 5in headlamps for the latter, whilst the standard cars had single 7in sealed beam units. Five grille slats were used on PCS and seven on the narrower grille PCD cars. A Griffin emblem was fitted centrally on the bonnet on deluxe cars, whilst base models had a full Vauxhall badge across the centre front, with less bright-work generally. Deluxe cars came with more ornate wheel trims (no longer the white side-wall tyres, though), and a deluxe badge was fitted to the right-hand side of the boot lid. Metalwork pressings were the same

The deluxe Cresta PC had twin headlamps. Use of whitewall tyres had been discontinued for the PC Crestas.

for both models. With not many to begin with, base model Crestas have become extremely rare.

Following adoption of the much better three-speed Strasbourg auto gearbox by 1970, the PC series continued in production until 1972, when the new FE Ventora adopted the same engine, effectively taking the PC's place as a larger-engined Vauxhall. There was some FE & PC overlap, with some late Crestas being registered in late 1972 under UK 'L' registrations, the popular Viscount stocks running empty earlier that year. End price for a late 1972 Cresta deluxe was £1266 in August 1972.

It is evident how wide the PCs were from this rear view of this early production example. In reality, 5ft 10in (allowing for a 15-gallon fuel tank) was massive in the mid-1960s.

The fully carpeted PC interior and all that dashboard wood ...

PC estate conversion

Martin Walter was once again commissioned to produce a very convincing-looking estate car on the new shape Cresta. This brand new model had a capacious boot (60ft^3 and 6ft 4in rear floor length with the rear seats folded flat). One 1967 example made its way to the Royal Household, and was UK-registered PYN1F.

Deliveries began in early 1966, and were based on the twin headlamp deluxe version. The rear-most side windows were surrounded by rubber, rather than the body colour used on the door glass, which gave an attractive add-on effect. As with previous Cresta (and Velox) estate conversions, the suspension was uprated, giving rise to a slightly higher ride height, and the existing rear lamp clusters were still used. Bigger section rear tyres were also fitted. When researching a previous Vauxhall book in 1990, the author saw photos in the Vauxhall archives of police prototypes of the estate conversion, performing motorway duties.

PC Viscount

Ford launched its top-specification Ford (Zodiac Mk4) Executive just after the sumptuous Viscount in 1966. The

The top-line Viscount dashboard with wood extended to the upper section.

Dagenham product was around £85 dearer than Luton's, and had only wind-down windows, but did have a sliding sunroof. The two cars were to compete head to head for around five years, and appealed to the same customer base. Another unlikely rival, the big Italian Fiat 2300, was around £130 cheaper.

Vauxhall's new lavish top Viscount (designated the PCE model) offered the following features over and above its Cresta stable-mates. Equipment and external trim: standard Powerglide auto transmission, high speed specification Avon Super Safety tyres,

The seamless lines of the Martin Walter-converted estate on the PC platform.

power brakes, black surrounds to headlamps, die-cast and squared extruded aluminium radiator grille, hand-drawn coach-lines on body-sides, grained vinyl roof covering, engine bay light and alternator fitted as standard.

Opulence inside: extra thick tufted carpets, full carpet with underlay in the boot and spare wheel cover fitted, folding picnic tables and elasticated pockets on rear of front seats, walnut door panels and extra sound insulation, reclining front seats with Chapman-Reutter hinges, reel-away safety belts, hide upholstery, power operated windows all round, electrically heated rear window, swivelling map-light, cigar lighter and glovebox lamp. Overall, an extra 1.3cwt was added, and the cost for all this? Just short of £400 over the standard Cresta deluxe, although £75 of this could be saved by deleting the Powerglide transmission feature and opting for the four-speed manual version.

Summing up, *Motorsport* magazine, in its 1967 test, stated that the Viscount "... may not appeal to enthusiasts but is a fine proposition for those who wish to combine spaciousness and comfort with the status symbol and who have less than £1500 to spend." The Viscount was discontinued along with its sister Cresta in early 1972. Its final list price had risen to £1705, a third more than the equivalent Cresta.

PC media advertising slogans

If you want a car that's more spacious, powerful, handsome and luxurious ... (Cresta)
11 good excuses for carving a Vauxhall Cresta (Cresta)
For an easy life, we built it the hard way (Cresta)
Never before such powered luxury in a £1500 car (Viscount)
When you drive yourself hard all day, why do it on the way home? (Viscount)
Viscount has it all. In plush (Viscount)
The safe, serene world of powered luxury (Viscount)
The breed's biggest and costliest. Viscount has it all. In plush (Viscount)
11 serious reasons for playing the power game (Viscount)

The Viscount cost considerably more than its PC sister cars. Note standard vinyl roof and unique front grille, power steering, brakes, windows and Powerglide transmission ...

PC BODY TYPES: four-door saloon, five-door estate: 1965-1972; **manufactured at**: Luton; **number produced**: Cresta PC 53,912, Viscount 7025.

PERFORMANCE: **top speed**: over 100mph (160kph); **0-60mph (100kph)**: 11 sec; **average economy**: 15mpg.

PRICE AT LAUNCH: £956 (Cresta, £1058 (Cresta deluxe), £1458 (Viscount).

MEASUREMENTS: **length**: 15ft 7in (4.7m); **width**: 5ft 10in (1.7m); **height**: 4ft 8in (1.4m); **wheelbase**: 8ft 11½in (2.7m); **weight**: 2796-3070lb (1268-139kg); **wheels**: 14in; **turning circle**: 34ft (10.36m); **fuel capacity**: 15 gallons (68 litres); **boot capacity**: 30ft^3.

TECHNICAL: **engine types**: 3293cc (six-cyl, petrol); **gearbox**: two-speed Hydra-Matic, three-speed auto, three-speed manual, optional overdrive; **suspension**: independent coil (front), variable rate semi-elliptic (rear); **brakes**: disc front, drum rear.

TRIM: Ambla, leather.

KEY OPTIONAL EXTRAS: Starmist metallic paint, alternator, leather seats, overdrive, fog lamps, leather upholstery on Cresta.

European influences: Chevette

Following the Geneva Motor Show and a press announcement in March 1975, and just as Tammy Wynette was topping the UK charts with her hit number one single *Stand By Your Man* in May 1975, The First Class – a little known group – released *Life Is Whatever You Want It To Be*, a huge and uplifting orchestral production with Tony Burrows' vocals. Vauxhall marketed the new Chevette on the back of a rewritten version of this song, sung by the same group. The catchy TV advert proclaimed "Whatever you do, whoever you are, go anywhere 'cos it's your kind of car. The Vauxhall Chevette – it's whatever you want it to be." It boasted about the car's multiple uses, including carrying family shopping, children, geese and even farmyard animals ... Sadly, the non-Vauxhall version of the song failed to make a position in the music charts. Perhaps the schedulers were worried it would give the Chevette extra unfair publicity, as the two songs sounded very similar and the Vauxhall version was popular all over commercial TV and cinema adverts?

A pre-production Chevette undergoes cold weather testing in north Europe before release.

An early entry level Chevette just after completion in 1975. Note the lack of a windscreen chrome surround.

The new 90mph Chevette was an entry level model based on a very much anglicised Opel Kadett C, available since 1973 when it replaced its 11-year-old predecessor. These were both part of the wide T-car floor-plan that emerged back in March 1970. Like the droop-snoot HP Firenza, the Chevette adopted the distinctive Pontiac Firebird-inspired sloping front end with unusual snow-catching recessed headlamps (these lasted until the 1980 model year, when they went flush with bigger lenses). Just two models were available: base and L. The base model was £150 dearer than the contemporary Viva standard two-door model, and a whopping £260 (nearly 20 per cent) dearer than the two-door Kadett GM cousin, so marketing had to be good to gain sales. Performance played a role here, with the Chevette being better than the bigger two-door Viva as it weighed in 95lb lighter, with more refined handling, too. It shared the same Viva UK mechanicals, save for the shortened propeller shaft.

An early Chevette hatch outside the Vauxhall factory in 1975.

A 1977 Chevette estate. The fuel filler was located on the nearside, whilst on the saloon it was on the driver's side.

A 1978 two-door Chevette L saloon.

Although many of its panels were similar to its Opel cousin's (the Kadett C was not marketed as a hatch from its early days, although the hatchback shape was familiar in Brazil since the T-car inception in 1973), the Chevette was hatchback only, with the saloons and estate (and van) coming a short while later. Initially, this clever idea kept the ranges distinctly apart, and further divisions were evident due to different paint options, alternative wheels, completely different dashboard and interior trim appointments, particularly the use of distinctive bold plaid cloth style seat trim in a variety of colours. Even the switchgear was different, the little Opels using the European system of wipers on the right stalk, indicators on the left stalk.

Although suspension setup was the same, engines and transmissions were different, too. The Chevette used the trusty new 1256cc block utilised in the HC Viva, whereas the Opel continued with the smaller and slower 1196 cc engine, with a smaller 1-litre unit available on the continent. Both models were sold alongside each other in the UK, although the GM sales brochures keenly kept them apart.

By the end of 1975, the Chevette GL appeared with sports wheels (shod with 175 x 70 SR tyres), rubber bumper over-riders, and a higher equipment level, including new centre console and velour interior door panels with door pockets. On the other end of the scale came the "limited production" (if the adverts were to be believed) Chevette E: an economy car at an entry price of just £1636.

Soon, however, those crossover models emerged, with Opel releasing its hatchback, the Kadett City, at the Frankfurt Motor Show in September 1975 and in February 1976

An early production four-door saloon. There were no hatches or estates on the four-door platform, although the US Chevrolet/Pontiac versions were offered in four-door hatch form.

A pre-face-lift Chevette hatch in GLS guise. Note black panel between the rear lamp clusters.

A metallic gold four-door Chevette L saloon built after the 1980 face-lift.

The tweed-style interior of a face-lifted four-door Chevette.

A Chevette GL face-lifted saloon with quite pronounced side rubbing strips that never quite suited the flow of the design.

The Chevette E two-door saloon from around 1981.

Revised wheels, those additional side rubbing strips and a fog lamp date this GL hatch to around 1982.

Recessed headlamps gave way to these larger, flush-fitting lamps in early 1980. This is a 1983-registered example photographed in 2022. It is regularly seen towing a caravan to car shows in Suffolk.

A no frills entry level hatch from around 1982, with no fuss steel wheels.

in the UK; to the untrained eye the penny dropped, as the two cars were indeed based on the same platform. A quick distant glance at the rear would tell them apart: Opels had the number plate fitted above the bumper, Vauxhalls fitted below.

By summer 1976, Vauxhall had introduced the two- and four-door saloon variants, followed by an estate car in September the same year. No five-door estate or hatchbacks were ever produced. In the USA, Chevrolet and Pontiac Chevettes were the only T-cars produced as five doors from 1978. The wider doors of the two-door saloons and hatchbacks were used, and the centre window on the side was front-hinged to open outwards to aid ventilation. All of these new models were based on the same wheelbase, with the extra length (10in) added after the rear axle. Whilst the handy hatch offered 12/34ft^3 of boot space (seats up/down), the new saloon gave 20ft^3, and the estate 33/53ft^3 (seats up/down). Confusingly, the petrol cap on the estate was on the opposite (UK passenger) side, and the spare wheel was mounted vertically on the right.

The same engine and transmission was offered across the entire range, which from June 1976 included a GLS derivative (along with the GL with chrome trim over the arches and along the sills – it even had a bonnet lamp ...), but this was deleted from the range in 1983. At this time, a rather-less-than base model E version was also marketed, staying on the new car price list until late 1982. In the first year of production, 65,000 Chevettes were built.

Chevette 2300HS

A rally version of the Chevette was developed with the help of Blydenstein Racing, which was responsible for Dealer Team Vauxhall. 400 2300HS Group 4 Homologation specials were announced as a future project late in 1976 for the 1977 new model scene via dealerships, although in the end nothing was available until spring 1978, at £5107.

Like its racing cousin, the road-going 2300HS sported wider but still rounded

Revised uprated cockpit of the 2300HS.

wheelarches, a massive glass-reinforced plastic front air dam and a rear spoiler, and the engine was the same slant-four shoehorned in from the Firenza, Magnum, Victor and VX4/90 models, with a new twin-cam 16-valve cylinder head. Suspension was from the Kadett 'C' GT/E, another successful rally car, and alloy wheels were fresh from Chevrolet. Similar to the Golf GTi trim style, almost tartan red-and-black bold plaid faced seats were fitted (the fronts with some extra bolstering), and, unlike the 1256cc cars, this trim theme was extended even to the door cards. This style of trim was also seen on the Magnum Sportshatch. Flashy red Vauxhall transfer graphics were fitted on the boot lid

A 1978 Chevette 2300HS with factory spoiler. The works rally cars had by now already made their debut. This press car was road taxed only until 1989.

A works rally car with the face-lifted hatch of 1980.

A Chevette 2300HSR photographed in 1990.

between the rear lamp clusters, and a large italic script 'HS' transfer emblem was added behind the conventional Chevette badge. The strobe decal stripes fitted were also carried over onto certain limited edition models in later years, but the 2300HS was further identified by extended red graphics that wrapped completely around the front and rear side windows. The cockpit bore a surprisingly close resemblance to 1256cc cars. The standard facia was retained, but with a rev counter replacing the fuel and temperature gauge dials. A new centre console housed these instruments, along with a voltmeter and oil pressure gauge. The 2300HS was only available in Silver Starfire metallic finish, and, with the bodykit, the revised model's Cd drag factor figure was reduced from 0.475 to 0.407.

The sales flyer listed full specification as: 16-valve twin-cam 2279cc engine, twin 175CD carburettors, 135bhp (DIN), an oil-cooler, five-speed gearbox, 6J alloy wheels with 205/6 OHR radial tyres, and rally-tuned suspension.

Following on from his 1974 Viva TV advert, 1976 F1 World Champion James Hunt also featured on the front cover of the March-May 1977 range catalogue, and in various contemporary magazine adverts. Vauxhall was quick to point out that he used a (1256cc!) Chevette as an everyday car. He also featured in a 1977 Chevette TV advert. For the Queen's Silver Jubilee in 1977 when a very limited run Chevette Jubilee with two-tone paintwork was produced.

Bill Blydenstein offered his tuning services to the smaller-engined cars, too. A front- and rear-spoilered, bored out, 1511cc car (registered MNM529P) was tested by *Autocar* and *Motorsport* in autumn 1977. It used the DTV Stage two-cylinder head and Lumenition electronic ignition, achieving 0-60mph in 11.4 seconds. Just after this, *Motorsport* got its hands on Pentti Airikkala's DTV Shepreth-built works car, RVA841S, for a full performance test. It proved to be the quickest rally car it had timed to that point, with a 0-60mph acceleration time of just 5.7 seconds ...

Two 1970s concept cars are worthy of note: Chevette Aero and Black Magic. The Chevette Aero, based on the 1976-78 Kadett C Aero at the time, sported a targa

The red Bold Plaid trim was used on the Chevette 2300HS & HSR, plus other late 1970s models.

top convertible roof, with overtones of the Fiat X1/9 and Triumph Stag. Two are reported to have been built as styling studies, and at least one of them survives. Maroon OVS72R has since been exported to the Netherlands, re-registered, and is in the safe hands of an enthusiast, still fitted with its distinctive red bold plaid cloth trimmed seats and matching 2300HS style red and black door cards, plus headrests.

The Black Magic concept car was displayed to an eager public at the 1979 UK Motor Show following a variety of previous guises. This was an all-black car designed and driven daily by GM design chief Wayne Cherry, who had reworked an early production 2300HS, RVD788R. It started life with a twin-cam head, but, after overheating issues partly caused by a very efficient front air dam, it was revised to a single cam cylinder head. It featured a striking black leather interior and 50/50 split folding rear seats, plus thicker carpets and a full-width wood dashboard following an extensive redesign. Extra storage was available on the gearbox tunnel. Unlike the HS, the extra ancillary gauges were mounted within the larger dashboard. The HS Getrag five-speed gearbox was fitted.

Focus, however, was on aerodynamics and drag co-efficient. Formula 1 racing and the Porsche 935/78 influences gave rise to deep side skirts that allowed a front end lift reduction of 52 per cent, whilst rear lift was reduced by 37.3 per cent, which led to greater straight line stability and improved high speed braking. Good luck jacking it up in the event of a puncture! Special rubber-skirted front and rear spoilers were also fitted to complete the overall package. Leading on from Black Magic, Mamos Garages of Greenford, West London, offered the HSX, another black offering with wood door cappings and dashboard based broadly on the 2300HS and Black Magic theme. Ten are reputed to have been built, with at least one known survivor, albeit reworked with a different engine.

In early 1980, the Chevette 2300HS vanished from the new price lists, bowing out at £5939: just over double the price of a base two-door model. The revised phase two Chevettes were made available early in 1980. These could be identified at a glance by the flush-fitting front headlamp lenses – which gave rise to better aerodynamics – and revised wheels. The saloon also sported bigger and very distinctive exterior side window demisters on the 'C' posts. Inside improvements included side window demisters on the dash, a driver's door pocket on the L version, and on both doors on the GL. Both of these trim specifications could now be ordered with automatic transmission, although it proved so sluggish it was rarely seen. Fuel economy was improved slightly with the help of the new Bosch distributor. In addition, rear seat legroom was increased a little following an initial criticism of the earlier models from taller journalists on contemporary road tests. At the same time, an E specification estate became available to join the existing L décor estate.

In April 1980, the 2300HSR was released: a further developed performance car that fared well in international Group B rallying events, easily identified by its very stylish Audi Quattro-style blister wheelarch extensions (this design also later adopted by the Nova three-door hatch). Affectionately nicknamed 'Plastic Fantastic' by *Autosport* magazine, due to its fibre-glass front and rear wings, spoiler bonnet and tailgate, 50 cars had to be completed to adhere to homologation rules, which was achieved by modifying a number of existing 2300HS vehicles. However, the new GM Dealer sport team rendered the vehicle obsolete, favouring the somewhat less exciting but nevertheless successful Manta 400.

1980 Chevette improvements

The 1980s marked the introduction of many limited editions in the car buying world, and the Chevette sneaked in a few before the end of its production, albeit with a little help from outside design houses.

The Chevette Special, a factory offering, was sold on the face-lifted four-door platform and included sports Rostyle wheels (à la the previous Magnum HC and later Chevette GL), metallic paint, push button radio, quartz clock, tinted glass, headrests and better trim from early 1980. Larry Dann, later famed from TV's *The Bill*, was employed on TV adverts to help publicise the new model. The Special was fitted with a raised rear boot badge manufactured similar to the Chevette badge, whereas later limited editions favoured transfer badging. Leading on from this, a rather splendid Sun Hatch limited edition was offered in summer 1980 on the three-door hatchback platform, just in time for UK 'W' registrations. This had a detachable glass sunroof, side repeaters on the wings, front headrests, plus the same tinted glass, sports wheels and metallic paint and interior appointments of the

The Sun Hatch Chevette was available for £3954 in the early 1980s.

The two-tone Chevette Special saloon brochure cover.

Black Magic. Note the Vauxhall transfer badge on the rear.

Chevette Special saloon versions. Both the Special and the Sun Hatch had a waist-height side body moulding along their flanks. Further Chevette Specials were made available in 1983 and boasted two-tone metallic paint. In addition, the 1981 Black Pear was another Chevette limited edition, available with ES specification, black paint and silver strobe stripes. The 1980 Ted Rogers-promoted (of TV's *3-2-1* fame) Command Performance hatchback was available in Hazel Brown or Silver Beige, alongside similar Cavalier and Carlton limited edition models of the same colour.

In early 1981, an Economy Special (ES) model was added to the new car line-up. Really basic specification cars were marketed extensively. Black bumpers, plastic seat trim (hard wearing 'vynide') and the deletion of a passenger visor was the stark reality, but both the two-door saloon and hatch could be bought brand new for well under £3000, which compared favourably to the all-new Vauxhall Astra.

Another limited edition included the £3999 1982 Silhouette with striking black paintwork and bumpers, twin mirrors, rear fog lamps, velour seats and interior, the front seats reclined and had matching head restraints too. A deletion of the chrome window surrounds added to the overall ghosted look, although standard chrome door handles remained. Like the 2300HS, some were available with strobe stripe decals (five red stripes of varying depth that followed the window contours and swept up at the back, and matched the red velour very well). These were also available in the early 1980s from SCV (Star Custom Vehicles) of Ampthill, Bedfordshire, 15 miles north of Vauxhall's factory at Luton. SCV stated it was Britain's leading independent creative styling and manufacturing specialists. It offered the Black Watch, Grenadier and LUX custom models. These attractive cars were hand-

One of half-a-dozen Blydenstein-prepped supercharged 2600cc Chevette HSRs, built well after Vauxhall's own Black Magic concept car.

finished limited editions and could be ordered with walnut dash and door cards, sports steering wheels, sunroofs, a unique hi-fi radio/cassette, metallic paint with special graphics and special custom wheels. Further limited edition hatchback Chevettes included the 125 Midnights and 75 Starlights, available from dealers in and around London and the Home Counties.

In September 1982, two years after the Astra joined the Vauxhall fleet, Chevette range rationalisation occurred and the basic E specification cars were dropped, followed by the deletion of the two-door L saloon, four-door GL saloon, and the GL hatch in August 1983.

Taking over in European GM sales after the Kadett C was discontinued (in favour of the new 1980 year model Kadett C – equivalent to the UK's Astra Mk1), 12,882 Chevettes were sold in Europe by Opel in left-hand drive form as its only rear-wheel drive small car. These must have been an odd sight alongside their former Opel Kadett C cousins, particularly as they carried neither Vauxhall or Opel badging. Indeed, the Chevette had been sold in a few European countries all along. French and Dutch brochures exist pre-face-lift, including the James Hunt leaflet of 1977.

After the aforementioned range rationalisation (only a Chevette four-door saloon and a three-door estate now existed), the Chevette finally stopped production and quietly disappeared in 1984, gently giving way to the year old Nova after some 415,608 units were produced, initially at Luton, then soon at the Ellesmere Port facility over a nine-year production run. The Chevette was the best selling UK hatchback from 1975-78.

Over in America, the Chevrolet Chevette soldiered on with the T-car theme (always as a hatch, but the Brazilian T-car sported a boot, van and estate bodies) until its final demise in 1987, after a 14-year run.

Bedford Chevanne

A half-ton payload Bedford Chevanne was also offered and was popular with many fleet buyers, its body lines sharing the same panels and flip-up tailgate as the estate, with identical power and transmission, including the rarely seen option of an automatic from 1980. Unlike the Astravan, no diesel version was ever offered.

Despite the Chevette styling being 12 years more modern than the Viva HA, somewhat unusually, the little Bedford HA van continued production, these boxy vans being regular sights in British Rail, British Gas and Royal Mail fleet service, and possibly more popular than the Chevanne – the HA had handy vertically split rear doors which proved popular. Effectively the Chevanne was killed off by the new Bedford Astravan. A Chevanne pick-up design made it to prototype form, but was never produced, although Daewoo sold a pick up on the T-car platform for the South Korean market, and in Uruguay the Grumett pick-up definitely had Chevette underpinnings, including the droopsnoot front end, replacing the HA-based Grumett pick-up of previous years.

Chevette media advertising slogans

Is it a sporty coupé, family saloon or handy estate?

It's whatever you want it to be

We'd like every family in Britain to be a three car family

What else does James Hunt drive? (saloon)

"I like driving my Chevette to work" James Hunt

You'll like what's happening at Vauxhall (saloon)

It's the Chevette you already know with that little bit more to like (GL)

Chevette wins Norwich grand prix (GL/GLS hatch)

It's the Chevette you already know, with that little bit more to like (GL)

Who says you can't afford a sporty coupé, a handy saloon and a family estate?

Chevette scoops Area Championship (saloon)

Have you noticed the way successful originals always get copied? (hatch)

We've changed very little, but improved quite a lot (face-lift)

Nothing drastic, just a few nice touches for 1980 (face-lift)

All the versatility of Chevette at a new low price (E)

The Bedford Chevanne utilised the body panels of the estate car. It was effectively replaced by the Astravan, although in the early 1980s (in terms of size at least) there was also the Bedford KB pick-up, Astravan and HA van.

The only belt you will have to tighten is this one (ES)
Before you buy a Chevette, consider the other half
Different shapes at the back, and all jolly nippy (Patrick McNee TV advert)
Get one while it's hot (Sun Hatch)
It's hard to beat a Chevette (HS)
Twin-cam twins (HS)
It brings out the Pentti Airikkala in you (HS)
The new champion (HS)
The car that takes the drag out of driving (Black Magic)
A lesson in aerodynamics (Black Magic)

CHEVETTE BODY TYPES: three-door hatchback, two-door saloon, four-door saloon, three-door estate, enclosed van: 1975-1984 (HS 1978-79, HSR 1980); **manufactured at**: Luton then Ellesmere Port; **number produced**: 415,608 including 400 (HS), 50 (HS/R).
PERFORMANCE: **top speed**: 90mph (148kph) (1256cc), 115mph (190kph) (HS); **0-60mph**: 13-17 seconds (1256cc), 8.5 sec (HS); **average economy**: 30-40mpg (1256cc), 20-23mpg (2300HS/R).
PRICE AT LAUNCH: £1593 (base model).
MEASUREMENTS: **length**: 12ft 11in (3.94m) (hatch), 13ft 9in (4.12m) (saloon, estate & van); **width**: 5ft 2¼in (1.58m); **height**: 4ft 4in (1.33m); **wheelbase**: 7ft 10¼in (2.39m); **weight**: 1821lb (826kg), 2235lb (1014kg) (HS/R); **wheels**: 13in (all models); **turning circle**: 30.2ft (9.2m) (1256cc), 31.3ft (9.52m) (HS/HSR); **fuel capacity**: 8.4 gallons/38.1 litres (hatch), 9.9 gallons/45 litres (saloon/estate); **boot capacity**: 7.6ft^3 (hatch), 17ft^3 (saloon), 53ft^3 (estate/van).
TECHNICAL: **engine types**: 1256, 2279cc, four-cyl petrol; **gearbox**: four-speed manual 1975-1984, automatic option from 1980, five-speed Getrag (HS/R); **suspension**: independent front coil springs, live axle coil springs at rear; **brakes**: disc front, rear drum.
TRIM: Vynide, cloth, tweed, dapple velour.
KEY OPTIONAL EXTRAS: tow bar, cigar lighter, rear seatbelts, sunroof, metallic paint, automatic transmission (from 1980).

The big V-cars: Carlton, Viceroy, Royale and Senator

Carlton (1978-86)

Just as the first Cavalier offered three years earlier had strong European connections with Opel, the new range of Carltons and luxury Royale models launched at the 1978 UK Motor Show were built alongside their Opel Rekord 'E' counterparts in Russelsheim, Germany, some 400 miles east of the Luton factory.

The Carlton was mildly anglicised for UK eyes, its most noticeable change being the adoption of the now familiar Vauxhall droop-snoot aerodynamic front end, which certainly set it apart from its German cousins. Eagle-eyed customers had already seen an early left-hand drive Opel Rekord at the UK Motor Show in 1977, as Opel insisted UK forces personnel could have ordered one for overseas use, thus circumnavigating the display rules for an early UK airing, much to the annoyance of the competition. Following the 1977 European launch of the new style Rekord, both cars were soon sold by GM within the UK, at least until 1982 when national changes occurred within the dealerships. Similarly, the luxurious Royale was almost a clone of the Opel Senator saloon and Monza coupé seen initially in May 1978.

Whilst the Rekord was available in two-door and four-door saloon, plus three- and five-door estate variants, Vauxhall kept its Carlton model range strictly to a four-door saloon version and the capacious five-door estate. Unlike Opel, which was selling its Rekord van in limited numbers in the UK, there was no commercial Carlton derivative. This hole in the market was left for the smaller Bedford HA, Chevanne and later Astravans. Effectively the Carlton was a larger replacement of the now rather ageing FE VX1800 and VX 2300 series, by then relatively uneconomical when comparing fuel consumption figures side by side. Indeed, the *Sunday Express* test of 12th November 1978 stated: "I would be most surprised if some Carlton owners do not claim this two-litre as the best economy since they persuaded their trusting offspring that the gas meter was a money box." Vauxhall was eager to boast about the luxury aspect of the new model, and the lavish sales catalogues did not disappoint.

The original Mk1 Carlton saloon.

Carlton Mk1 estate, pre-face-lift.

The Opel Rekord van is a close enough representation of what a Bedford Carlton van might have looked like.

All Carltons (and indeed Royales) featured very sturdy and heavy chrome bumpers with strong rubber strips and strong square block over-riders, seemingly identical (but incompatible) as the Royale featured longer body dimensions. For overall length, the UK-badged cars were very slightly longer due to these massive, almost Volvo proportion rubber over-riders.

Apart from obvious badge changes,

the Vauxhall and Opel models were almost identical save from different colour and trim options in 2-litre form (the Opel Rekord also came with 1.7-, 1.9-litre petrol engines and a couple of diesels on the continent). The red, beige, blue or black ribbed velour cloth interiors were complemented by a dashboard and door cards of the same colour, in true 1970s fashion ... The Mk1 Carlton saloon and estates continued largely unchanged until September 1981, which saw the introduction of new steel wheels, body colours and Venezia velour trim, plus completely revised dashboard layouts (similar to the Royale models with a 'step down' on the passenger side), including the Royale four-spoke steering wheel.

In four years, the price had risen from launch £5627/£6197 (saloon/estate), to £6853/£7161 (1.8-litre/2.0-litre) saloon, £7530/£7791 (1.8-litre/2.0-litre) estate in November 1982 when major revisions to the phase two Carlton were made. There was an available upgrade to a new GL version, which commanded an extra £400, offering a tiltable four-spoke steering wheel, central door locking and headlamp wash/wipe. A top line CD came with tilting/sliding sunroof, Turin velour cloth trim extending to the door cards and front and rear head restraints, manual rear suspension levelling system, and pencil-beam halogen headlamps, plus digital audio came onboard in 1983, with the saloon pitched at £9039.

Bringing it further inline with the Opel Rekord (now type designated E2), the differences between the face-lifted models became negligible. Gone was the characteristic droop-snoot nose in favour of polycarbonate grey bumpers and spoiler, new wheels, revised body side mouldings etc., and the traditional Vauxhall bonnet flutes that had been around for decades finally disappeared. Paying an extra £400 for the economy, a 2.3-litre diesel power unit was also offered (with its obligatory bonnet bulge), as well as an optional smaller four-cylinder 1.8-litre overhead cam petrol engine that helped out with savings on company car taxation revenue. At motor show time in 1984, the 2-litre was replaced by a 2.2-litre fuel injected engine, which shaved over a second from the 0-60mph time, to a commendable 10.3 seconds. The public loved it, as did company car executives. In 1983, new shape Carlton sales hit 17,156, compared to the earlier model's 4603 in 1982: up by 372 per cent. Sales actually peaked for the Carlton in 1984, with 20,184 units sold.

The 76ft^3 (rear seats folded) estate was cavernous, wider (at 52 inches) than the Volvo 245 of the time. It offered 77 inches with the 50/50 split rear seats folded down, and it sold well. Advertising was perhaps aimed at the (more expensive) Range Rover and Volvo 245/265 set, with the slogan "100 horses in front. Room for the hounds behind". With room, apparently, for two six-footers to bed down! Unlike Volvo, Peugeot or Citroën, Vauxhall never marketed a rear-facing third row of seats, however, despite them being popular with young families.

This phase two version of the original Carlton lasted until the tail end 1986 and ran with L, GL and CD derivatives on both saloons and estates. They were superseded by the inception of the completely new 1986 generation models, also sold as the Opel Omega overseas.

Royale

Launched alongside the Carlton were the luxuriously appointed, all independently sprung Royale models: the saloon, at £8354, was almost identical to the Opel Senator, and the dearer coupé, at £8662, was close cousin to the new Monza fastback, both way more expensive than the Carlton. The brochures were keen to point out that everything was included as standard, with only air-conditioning remaining a major option. "It has everything you could unreasonably demand," headlined the magazine adverts.

Originally, the somewhat garish interior colours such as red and blue were marketed; there was a less striking beige, but the Monza had an even louder bright green offered! The mainly automatic 138hp 2.8-litre carburettor model continued unchanged until an optional 180hp 3.0-litre fuel injected car in late 1980 which followed the option of a new five speed manual transmission type. All-round disc brakes were standard. The brochures pointed out "Deep, luxurious seats upholstered in rich velour, deep-pile carpet and elegant décor and fittings make riding in a Royale, Senator or Monza the height of gracious travel." 14in alloy wheels were the norm (the Monza had larger 15in units). This was Vauxhall's tool in moving upmarket. Vauxhall sent a circular to the dealers stating it should only be sold to "Higher

The opulent Royale saloon was only to be sold to more affluent members of society if Vauxhall's guidance to dealers was rigorously followed ...

The Royale coupé: initially 2.8-litre, then optional 3-litre like its Opel Monza cousin.

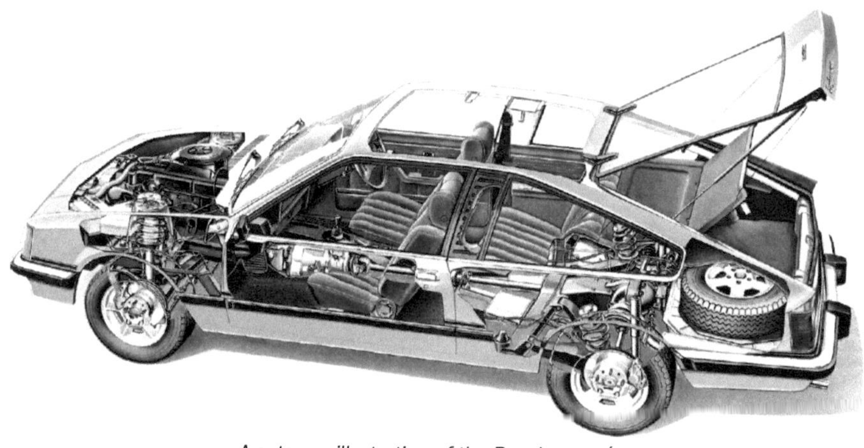

A cutaway illustration of the Royale coupé.

and intermediate managerial, administrative or professionals," and not to just anybody, regardless of whether they could afford it ... These cars were thirsty: whilst the automatics were better around town, the manual versions were 10 per cent more economical on a run (the absolute best available was 34.9mpg at a constant 56mph for a five-speed manual 3-litre saloon, the worst, 17.1mpg urban figure for the same car).

At the same time as the Carlton phase two face-lift, the Royales (and six-cylinder Opels) also received a new cockpit-style dashboard layout and the rather dated velour trim was replaced by a more conservative range of trim options. Rear seat passengers could now enjoy their own heating vents, and the Viceroy style front bib spoiler was also added, but alas, imports of the Royale from the German factory ceased in February 1982.

The 1981 Viceroy given to the author to restore when writing a previous Vauxhall book.

The same car, rear aspect. It had the nose of the Royale with the tail of the Carlton. Just 2295 were sold.

Viceroy

An odd-ball in the line-up was the silky-smooth 114hp 2.5-litre six-cylinder Viceroy, almost identical to the fuel-injected 130hp Opel Commodore C, which sat firmly in the Vauxhall price range between the Carlton and the Royale. To ease any confusion, the weekly press ran double page black and white Vauxhall adverts that explained precisely where the Viceroy was in the current line-up. Essentially, it had the longer nose of the Royale, whilst retaining the rear lines of the Carlton. It was quickly identified by its striking white cross on a satin matt black grille (à la VX4/90), which took its mouldings from the contemporary Royale.

The rear suspension was not independent, as utilised by its upmarket stablemates, and, despite its high price, tinted glass was still optional. Only a saloon was marketed, although a unique estate version was manufactured in 1981 for the Royal Household, which still exists in the hands of an enthusiast. Over on the continent, however (and indeed in Australia with Holden cars offering up to 4.2-litre V8s), an estate version was indeed sold. Four-speed manuals (with optional electronic overdrive) plus three-speed automatics were offered, all with strobe decal side stripes. It was both smoother and sprightlier than the Carlton, not by a huge margin, but fuel consumption suffered and only 2295 were sold, making it one of the rarest ever Vauxhall production cars. In its 4th July 1981 group test of an overdrive manual Viceroy, Rover SD1 2600S, Granada 2.8i and Volvo 244 GLT, *Motor* magazine stated: "The sleek shovel nose of the Viceroy, however, can do little to compensate for its comparative lack of power in this company, and it emerges as the slowest car, both on top speed (108.1mph) and with a 0-60mph time of 10.7 sec, standing start acceleration." Sadly even Vauxhall gave it no mention in its *Vauxhall Story* (Education Service), edition 8, of August 2002.

Although only available for two years, in its later, rarer form the Viceroy shared the revised Carlton dashboard, somewhat

A face-lifted Mk1 Carlton CD from 1984. At the time it was known as the Carlton 2, but was essentially a modified bodyshell version of the Mk1 cars.

A face-lifted Mk1 Carlton estate; this with the 2.3-litre diesel engine, as evidenced by the bonnet bulge.

toned-down Venezia interior colours trims, cloth door inserts, four new exterior colours, a front bib spoiler, electronic ignition and more aerodynamic remote-controlled door mirrors. The electronic overdrive was now standardised, too. One popular, good-looking option was BMW lookalike alloy wheels. Viceroys used five-stud wheels like the Royales, whereas the Carltons were four-studded until the next generation in 1986.

This revised version did not last long on the Royale and Viceroy. These models were quite rare in the UK, lasting in production for only a few months until the face-lifted Carlton was introduced. The Viceroy was last offered at £9556 (it started life at £7863 and the price increased heavily), and disappeared from the price lists in November 1982, with the Royale saloon 2.8-litre at £12,257 and range topping coupé (with optional 3.0-litre) at £14,060.

The run-out models were heavily discounted, as late car depreciation was high and many were Luton registered. The Opel Senator A and Monza continued alongside, and these cars were also heavily face-lifted when the phase two Carlton was introduced, similarly with plastic bumpers, albeit now body-coloured.

For clarity, the Monza continued until 1987, with the slightly lowered GSE replacing the 3.0 E in spring 1984. Although never available with Vauxhall badging, it was a true enthusiast's car with LCD dashboard, tiltable steering wheel, spoilers, darkened wheels and rear lamps, and of course, that stylish Recaro seating.

Senator A

The Opel Senator, around since 1978, also enjoyed the 1982 face-lift and was available on the continent as both a 2-litre base model with plastic wheel trims, and a 2.3-litre diesel complete with the bonnet bulge. Overseas conversions included long-wheelbase ambulances, hearses and a rather splendid Keinath estate conversion plus their own longer wheelbase executive model. In autumn 1984, for the UK at least, the Senator was rebadged as a Vauxhall, now its top 3.0i CD model priced at £14,565, with standard sunroof, air-conditioning, heated front seats and the Monza's LCD dashboard. The entry level model 2.5i was £11,372, also carried over from the previous Opel line-up. The double page advertising slogan proudly read "Vauxhall proudly offer you a Ghia change," a great play on words referencing the top Ford models of the day.

An interesting new option was ABS braking. By the end of production, three UK garages in the Birmingham area were offering Polar White, five-speed, 3-litre manual Senators with heavy-duty battery and alternators. These had been destined for the police force, but were surplus to requirement, and sold from just £10,995 plus taxes. Just 2751 Vauxhall Senators were sold in 1986. An interesting but little-known fact: over 80 V-cars were converted to Ferguson Formula four-wheel-control throughout the 1980s (mainly

A clever play on words for the new Senator press advert of 1985.

between 1980 and 1982) by the UK's FF Developments, apart from eight Bitter models (a sports car based on the Opel platform), the rest were all Opel badged, and it is generally assumed they were for military application.

The sumptuous rear compartment of the Senator.

V-car 1978-85 media advertising slogans

Vauxhall present a car of distinction (Carlton)
Have you heard the whisper? (Carlton)
As you might gather from the name, the car is roomy, comfortable and rather stylish (Carlton)
Relief from back trouble (Carlton estate)
100 horses in front. Room for the hounds behind (Carlton estate)
Fly in luxurious comfort (Carlton face-lift)
Sitting room at the front. Spare room at the back (Carlton face-lift estate)
Royale performance (Royale)
It has everything you could unreasonably demand (Royale)
Luxury is built in, not bolted on (Royale)
Very, very occasionally a great new car is launched (Royale)
A level of luxury that's fast disappearing (1983 Monza)
Seats four in comfort, leaves the rest standing (Monza GSE)
It also shows the Monza is ahead of other luxury coupés (Monza GSE)
If it's your job to know about cars, how much do you know about the new Vauxhall Viceroy (Viceroy)
What price individuality? (Viceroy, Royale & Carlton)
The luxurious new Vauxhall Senator
Vauxhall proudly offer you a Ghia change

The author and his left-hand drive Senator estate conversion, bought in Holland in 1997.

V-CAR (1978-86) BODY TYPES: four-door saloon, three-door coupé, five-door estate: 1978-1986; **manufactured at**: Luton & Russelsheim; **number produced**: 80,000 Carlton, 7119 Royale, 2295 Viceroy, 33,125 Senator (including Mk2).
PERFORMANCE: **top speed**: 107/130mph (175/215kph) (Carlton 2-litre/Senator 3-litre); **0-60mph (100kph)**: 11.2/10.5 sec; **average mpg**: 17-25mpg (six-cyl cars), 23-30mpg (four-cyl cars).
PRICE AT LAUNCH: £4600 (Carlton) £8354 (Royale).
MEASUREMENTS: **length**: 15ft 6in/4.72m (Carlton), 15ft 7in/4.74m (Viceroy/Royale coupé), 17ft/5.18m (Royale saloon/Senator); **width**: 5ft 8in (1.72m); **height**: 4ft 3½in (1.30m) except Senator – 4ft 5in (1.35m); **wheelbase**: 8ft 9in (4.34m) Carlton, Viceroy & Royale coupé, 8ft 9½in (4.5m) Senator; **weight**: 2492/2602lb (1130/1180kg) Carlton saloon & estate, 2712lb (1230kg) Viceroy, 3164/3175lb (1435/1440kg) Royale saloon & coupé; 3045lb (1384kg) Senator; **wheels**: 14in; **turning circle**: 32ft 6in/9.9m (Carlton), 32ft 10in/10m (Viceroy & Royale), 32ft 4in/9.85m (Senator); **fuel capacity**: 14.3 gallons/65 litres (Carlton saloon & Viceroy), 15.4 gallons/70 litres (Carlton estate & Royale coupé), 16.5 gallons/75 litres (Royale saloon & Senator); **boot capacity**: 17ft^3 (Viceroy & Carlton), 17.7ft^3 (Royale saloon & Senator), 26.5ft^3 (Royale coupé), Carlton estate: 31/76ft^3 (seats up/down).
TECHNICAL: **engine types**: 1796, 1979, 2197cc, four-cyl, 2490cc, 2784cc, 2986cc, six-cyl, petrol, 2260cc, four-cyl diesel; **gearbox**: four- & five-speed manual, three- & four-speed automatic; **suspension**: independent MacPherson coil all models at front, live axle coil rear (Carlton & Viceroy), independent coil rear (Royale & Senator); **brakes**: front disc, rear drum (Carlton & Viceroy), rear disc (Royale & Senator).
TRIM: cloth, ribbed velour.
KEY OPTIONAL EXTRAS: automatic transmission, overdrive, power steering, tinted glass, sunroof, alloy wheels, air-conditioning, tow bar.

Carlton 2

Enter late 1986, when Vauxhall pulled the wraps off its brand new generation 'jelly mould' Carltons. This new low-drag bodied model (Cd factor 0.28) was again available as a four-door saloon plus cavernous five-door estate car in a wide variety of trims and engine specifications primarily aimed at the middle-management executive market. The advert headline "We are delighted but not surprised" was published in January 1987, as the new Carlton was awarded Car of the Year 1987 by an independent jury of 57 European motoring journalists. The main features were intelligent all-round suspension, flush fitted

A second generation Carlton GL saloon.

glass, retractable windscreen wipers, and had electronic self-levelling headlamp system. This was a brand new design, well away from the previous Carltons. Contemporary press adverts stated "More and more families are switching to the Carlton estate," a direct pop at ever-safety-first Volvo with its ageing 240 and new 700 series estates, boasting what Volvo did not have: ACT – Advance Chassis Technology. This new technology apparently "... helped against fishtailing and spinning," things that could lead to an accident scenario under heavy breaking and corrective steering. In the descriptive Vauxhall press adverts showing a car swerving in an emergency, the cat lived!

Initially available with just 1.8- and 2-litre petrol-engined variants, plus the 2.3-litre diesel-powered car, the range was later boosted to include a dual-ram 2.6i and the 3000 GSi (first 12v then 24v) and Lotus Carlton 3.6-litre, described shortly.

Prior to the inception of the later Omega in 1994, the Carlton still utilised two bodyshells and had a somewhat revised look, the top model being the 3-litre 24v Diamond estate with auto gearbox as standard, now £26,465. Additional models such as the Carlton Diplomat were marketed along the way with cruise control, air-conditioning, leather seats and a richly grained walnut interior. These were the days of ten discs in a boot-mounted CD auto changer, and six speakers. It was dubbed

An early second generation Carlton GL saloon.

"The Luxury Cruiser with First Class Cabin," by the marketing department. Other models included the Plaza (saloon only), Club and Voyager (estates only), L, GL, CD, CDX, GSi, and later the Lotus.

Top of the line was a seemingly bullet-proof GSi 3000 sports model, first seen in March 1987, which always looked best in black or red, especially with its prominent rear spoiler. The awesome single-built Carlton Thundersaloon, a regular sight on the track, was utilised in period advertisements for the 3000 GSi to whet the appetite for potential buyers. For an extra £1800, an optional 24v part-leather seated 3000 GSi became

A 1992 CD Carlton estate.

A 1991 Carlton Diplomat.

Interior of the Carlton Diplomat.

available in November 1989, with a further 27hp and double the number of valves. The GSi had vanished from the new car price lists by the end of 1992, last offered at £25,000 (24v only). The more powerful engine was also offered in top line Senators, too, bringing a sub 8 second 0-60mph time.

Lotus Carlton

The Holy Grail of Vauxhalls just has to be the twin charge-cooled Garrett T25 turbo-charged Lotus Carlton, a stunning hand-built four-door 3.6-litre supercar that ate other early 1990s super saloons for breakfast. With power delivered via a Corvette ZR-1 six-speed manual gearbox, amazingly it could accelerate from 0-60mph and come to a complete standstill again in just under 9 seconds! Announced late in 1989 at the UK Motor Show to an eager public, alongside the new Calibra with a preview brochure handout displaying a left-hand drive pre-production car, it was not until late 1990 that the eager road testers got their hands on an example, and only 950 were produced: the Lotus Carlton (around 320 cars) and, for overseas, the Lotus Omega (around 630 left hookers). It was certainly controversial, and questions were being asked in the Houses of Parliament (by Alex Carlile) about getting the car banned from sale to the public. UK newspaper headlines were written asking what the point was of such speed (it had at least a 180mph top-end), and the motoring media heavily compared it to the (arguably) better handling BMW M5. This was a time when top German manufacturers were restricting top speeds to 155mph, but the Lotus remained unrestricted. And all this for £48,000 back in 1990! Today, good clean secondhand examples command a decent price, with some examples being pulled from specialist auctions well before sale time, having been sold privately.

The mighty Lotus Carlton was shod with wide 235/45 ZR 17in tyres and came in a unique Imperial Green with Connolly leather seats, centre console, door cards and facia trim. Maximum power was a mouth watering 365ps at 5000rpm. The Motor Show handout stated it was "A perfect fusion of ideals and technologies," and land speed record holder Richard Noble road-tested an example for *Autocar & Motor* magazine in 1990, stating that the most memorable part of the Lotus

Stretched versions of the Carlton were available for funeral parlour and limousine use.

Carlton was the brakes, and that they were simply the best he had ever tried on a road car.

Carlton 2 media advertising slogans

It's about to put the skids under its rivals
The first class cabin (Diplomat)
The luxury cruiser (Diplomat)
Why not glide to work? (CDX)
Driving a luxury car is less taxing with a Carlton CDX
Nine out of ten cats prefer Carltons
We are delighted, but not surprised
Take the winner for a lap of honour
A suspension system so advanced, it even helps you unwind
We've not only loaded the car, but also the argument for buying it (estate)
More and more families are switching to the Carlton estate
Now you know why so many Porsche 944s are bright red (GSi)
Earth moving equipment (GSi)
Doesn't drive like one, doesn't even look like one, doesn't one seem like a good idea? (3.0i CDX estate)
Loch Ness drained (Thundersaloon)
Precious Few (Lotus Carlton)
1st 1st 1st (Calibra, 24v Carlton & Lotus Carlton)

The GSi 3000 24v Carlton was good for nearly 150mph in the days when advertising happily boasted about such topics ...

The Lotus Carlton, was three times the price of a standard Carlton, but £48,000 bought similar performance to the contemporary £120,000 Ferrari 512 road car. However, the Lotus Carlton could transport five people and their luggage ...

Interior appointments of the Lotus Carlton. Note the fine leather and the six speed gearlever.

CARLTON 2 BODY TYPES: four-door saloon, five-door estate: 1986-1994; **manufactured at**: Russelsheim; **number produced**: 241,051 (including 320 UK Lotus Carltons).
PERFORMANCE: **top speed**: 121-149mph (200-245kph); **0-60mph (100kph)**: 10.8/7.0 sec (1.8-litre/GSi 24v compared), Lotus Carlton, see text; **average economy**: 24-35mpg.
PRICE AT LAUNCH: £14,183 (2-litre), £48,000 (Lotus Carlton).
MEASUREMENTS: **length**: 15ft 4½in (4.69m) saloon, 15ft 6¼in (4.73m) estate; **width**: 5ft 10in (1.78m); **height**: 4ft 10in (1.47m); **wheelbase**: 8ft 11½in (2.73m); **weight**: 2714lb/1244kg (2-litre); **wheels**: 14in (17in on Lotus); **turning circle**: 34ft 5in (10.5m); **fuel capacity**: 16.5 gallons (75 litres) saloon, 15.4 gallons (70 litres) estate; **boot capacity**: 18.4ft^3 (saloon), 65ft^3 (estate seats down).
TECHNICAL: **engine types**: 1796cc, 1998cc, four-cyl, 2594cc, 2969cc, 3615cc, six-cyl, petrol, 2260cc four-cyl diesel; **gearbox**: five-speed manual (Lotus six-speed only), four-speed auto; **suspension**: independent MacPherson coil (front), independent coil (rear); **brakes**: disc all round.
TRIM: cloth, velour, leather
KEY OPTIONAL EXTRAS: various on each model including tow bar, uprated radio system, air-conditioning etc.

Senator B

The new range of Senators was announced late in spring 1987. With its cheese-cutter front grille, the new 'jelly mould' Senator B (also available from Opel at the same time, as was the norm) made its press debut that May. It utilised the 2.5- and 3.0-litre straight-six engines. This was an expensive gamble for GM, taking some £700 million and six years to produce, to rival the Rover 800, BMW 7-series, Volvo and Audi. Production was again in Germany. Advertising was aimed at company directors, and it became the chairman's choice of car; the adverts boasted "The engine is so quiet you can almost hear the computer talking to it ..." and "Engineered for unruffled grace ..." Vauxhall media encouraged dealers to advertise the car in local business press and country style magazines, to emphasise its exclusivity.

The top-line Vauxhall quickly replaced the ageing Senator in both manual and automatic form. The price points were £14,830 (2.5-litre) to £19,820 (top 3.0-litre OD model), this aggressive pricing certainly made the new car good value for money. It drove like a dream, with really light controls, and, with its quiet charm and surprising economy helped by its sleek lines, became too easy to break the speed limit in (particularly the 24v version ...).

Notable appointments included a refrigerated glovebox, six-way fully adjustable driver's seat, electronic ride control, and several computers. The gearbox had three modes of operation: 'Winter' (which started in third gear to avoid wheelspin), 'Economy' (everyday use) or 'Power' (which allowed higher revs for better acceleration).

The CD model gained the Caravan Club's Towcar of the Year award in 1988. A team of testers put 24 new cars through their paces, with the Senator CD beating them all hands-down. Favourable comments were directed at its electronic ride height system, electronic adjustable auto gearbox settings, powerful brakes and strong engine.

By the end of 1989, a reworked 24v 3-litre engine version had been added to the top of the range, identified by its twin rectangular tailpipes and small boot-mounted 24v badge. This new engine had a dual-ram variable intake system and twin catalysts. Manual transmission was still optional, good for 149mph. The futuristic LCD dashboard was not part of the 24v's specification, the more conservative analogue dials of the lesser models were adopted instead (although the mid-1990 *Autocar & Motor* magazine early road test car, G465XNM, was fitted with LCD instrumentation). The 3.0 CD and 24v came with alloy wheels, whereas the lesser models had flush-itting plastic wheel covers. A 150hp 2.6-litre engine replaced the 140hp 2.5-litre for mid-1991 model year.

By September 1992, the Senator range had lost the standard 3.0i and 3.0i CD models, rationalised down to just the (enlarged from 2.5) 2.6i and 3.0i 24v. This long distance cruiser lasted seven years until 1994, moving aside for the new 3-litre V6 top-end Omegas, bailing out with just the last 204PS 3.0i 24v CD model left, offered at £27,400.

Senator B media advertising slogans

The engine is so quiet you can almost hear the computer talking to it

The Chairman's statement

"At £20,000 I'd expect at least two of everything. So be it"

Another day, another gearbox

If it had two engines, where's the other one? (24v)

SENATOR B BODY TYPES: four-door saloon: 1987-1994; **manufactured at**: Russelsheim; **number produced**: 69,943. **PERFORMANCE**: **top speed**: 149mph (245kph) 24v; **0-60mph (100kph)**: 7.7 sec; **average economy**: 25-30mpg (3-litre 24v). **PRICE AT LAUNCH**: £14,830-£19,820. **MEASUREMENTS**: **length**: 15ft 10½in (4.84m); **width**: 5ft 9½in (1.76m); **height**: 4ft 8½in (1.44m); **wheelbase**: 8ft 11½in (2.73m); **weight**: 3374lb (1530kg);

The second generation Senator was also built in Germany alongside the Opel version. This is a 1992 Vauxhall model.

wheels: 15in; **turning circle**: 32ft 5in (9.88m); **fuel capacity**: 16.5 gallons (75 litres); **boot capacity**: 18.7ft^3.
TECHNICAL: **engine types**: 2490cc, 2594cc, 2969cc, six-cyl petrol; **gearbox**: five-speed manual, four-speed auto; **suspension**: independent MacPherson coil (front), independent progressive rate coil (rear); **brakes**: disc all round.
TRIM: velour, leather.
KEY OPTIONAL EXTRAS: manual transmission no cost.

The 24v badging and twin rectangular exhausts featured on this model only. The rear lamp clusters on the Senator 'B' must be about the biggest that Vauxhall/Opel had produced. The 24v model had a smoked glass effect ...

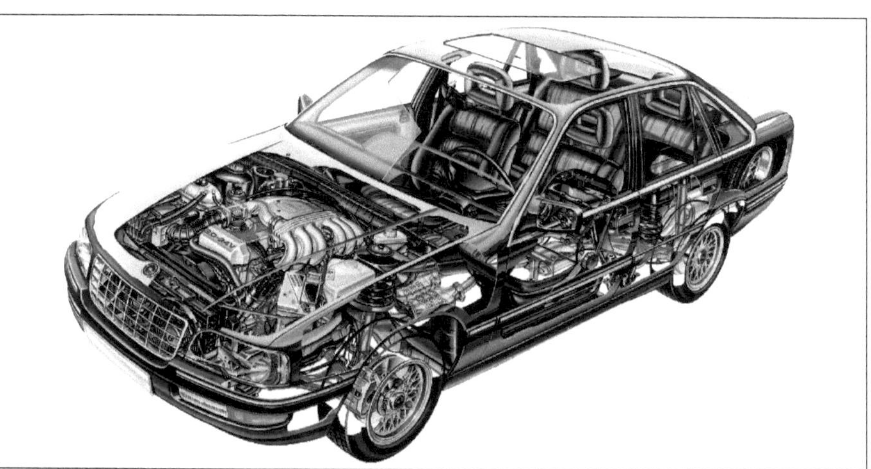

Cutaway illustration of the 24v Senator.

One of several press adverts for the second generation Senator.

1975-1994 family wheels: Cavalier Mk1, 2 and 3 plus Calibra

Cavalier Mk1

The Cavalier range quietly arrived just ahead of the 1975 London Motor Show, and, following the Chevette, it was the second mainstream Vauxhall model based on Opel engineering; the all-new Ascona saloon and Manta coupé being the donors. Effectively, this was the first Opel to wear a Vauxhall badge. Recently completed Cavaliers were rushed to the Earl's Court Show at very short notice following a quick local hotel press launch. All models adopted the now familiar droop-snoot front, which was also used, albeit in revised form, on the Opel Manta. The Ascona saloon favoured a conventional vertical grille.

Initially, two-door and four-door saloons were offered in 1.6- and 1.9-litre derivatives, plus an attractive Manta-based 1.9-litre coupé notchback with side opening rear quarter glass. No estate cars were ever produced, either in the UK or on the continent. The doors on the two-door derivative were slightly longer to allow easier access to the rear compartment.

The Cavalier coupé was certainly a departure from the norm. Contemporary Vauxhall magazine advertising boasted: "Turning heads come as standard ... Scores of eyes follow your progress along the High Street. Others peek at your registration, expecting initials and a low number. Such is the appeal ..." This was Vauxhall's entry into the medium coupé market, and the car, although highly geared, immediately proved popular. Aside from the badging, the only noticeable difference from the Opel Manta was the adoption of a bib spoiler up front and lack of any slits on the front droop-snoot section. Surprisingly, there was no rev counter on the GL specification; odd in that, given the high gearing, it was easy to red-line the engine at the 110mph top speed (where allowed).

The GL was recognisable on the outside by a black body moulding with chrome insert, plus bright-work trim on the wheels and arches and along the bottom of the sills.

The Cavalier Mk1 four-door saloon.

The Cavalier Mk1 two-door saloon.

Press advert for the Cavalier Mk1 coupé.

A major difference in the interior was the more comprehensive dashboard instrumentation and velour trim instead of cloth. The cars sold steadily, but did not compete as well as hoped in the fleet sector against Ford's Cortina.

A Cavalier Mk1 coupé at the Luton works.

A Cavalier Mk1 Sports Hatch. Its name appeared as two distinct words on the 'B' post, see inset.

The hardy Viva/Chevette 1256cc engine and gearbox combination was offered in 1300 L specification only, when Antwerp production moved to Luton from August 1977. In March 1978, the cam-in-head 1.9-litre engine was bored out to 2-litres, which improved power output and improved performance figures. In September that year, to take the Capri II and Capri III head on, a tail-gated Sports Hatch (GL or new GLS trim model) joined the range, which created a fourth bodyshell based very much on the Wayne Cherry Project 1 prototype. Unlike the coupé, this was offered in both 1.6-litre and 2-litre forms, and at last the GLS came with a rev counter. This was a Cavalier, the adverts stated, that was "... not a car to cross swords with ..." These versions were not built in the UK, but in Belgium, alongside Opel Mantas and Asconas.

Interior of Cavalier Mk1.

Neither coupé nor Sports Hatch appeared as official badging on the boot panels of the Mk1 Cavalier, but small 'Sports Hatch' motifs appeared at the bottom of the 'B' pillars on such models. Tuner Bill Blydenstein offered a 2.4-litre, bored-out, turbo-charged version of the Sports Hatch for an extra £1300 or so, which shaved an extra second off the 0-60mph time but retained a similar top speed.

By summer of 1979, a new 2000 GLS four-door saloon was also offered, fitted with tinted glass, a rev counter, velour trim, push-button radio with stereo cassette, passenger door mirror and a black vinyl roof as standard. Worthy options included metallic paint, automatic transmission, sliding steel sunroof and unique alloy road wheels.

To help with fleet sales, a 1.6-litre LS saloon was introduced in June 1980, extended to include a 2-litre in the October. A campaign followed comparing the attributes of the LS to that of the Mk5 Cortina, in an attempt to pull some extra fleet sales. At this time the L décor model was offered with the Chevette bold plaid seat trim. By September 1981, the Mk1 Cavalier was phased out to make way for the new front-wheel-drive Cavalier Mk2s.

Cavalier Mk1 Specials

Not many special model Cavalier Mk1s were produced. Those that were included the £4162 Silver Special 1600 two-door in early 1980 with blue plaid cloth trim, body side mouldings, sports style wheels and metallic silver paintwork. The £5128 Command Performance, based on the LS but with 2-litre power, was sold in conjunction with similarly badged Carltons and Chevettes. It was offered in Hazel Brown or Silver Beige, with tinted glass and remote driver's door mirror. Between January and May 1980, the model was promoted by Ted Rogers of TV's *3-2-1* fame at various venues across the UK. Contrastingly, the Centaur was a stylish £7103 cabriolet model marketed by Crayford Cars and based on the coupé platform. Such a model took pride of place on the 1977 Vauxhall UK Motorfair stand, taking over perhaps where the by now obsolete Triumph Stag had left a gap in the T-top cabriolet market, with the marketing department stating that it was the stiffest soft-top car available in 15 years.

The Silver Aero Sports Hatch concept car still appears at classic car events today.

In 1980, a Cavalier Sports Hatch was used as a basis for a one-off Wayne Cherry Vauxhall styling exercise, and displayed at the 1980 UK NEC Motor Show. The Silver Aero utilised unique alloy wheels with wide (for the time) 215 section tyres, special customised air pumpable Recaro seats with electrically-operated backrests, new interior materials and a very keenly designed paintwork package to create a state of the art-looking vehicle. The outer fibre-glass panels were so designed that the car offered a drag co-efficient of just 0.292, making it possibly the most aerodynamic vehicle on the road. Similar to the Ford X-Pack programme, panels were also planned to be sold by Vauxhall Sportpart dealers as easily screwed or bolt-on aftermarket items (no need for filler or paint), save for the air-ducted fibre-glass bonnets, but the imminent introduction of the Mk2 Cavalier precluded this. As with the Black Magic Chevette, jacking up the vehicle caused a real headache! Power came from a rebored 2-litre cam-in-head unit, uprated to 2.4-litre TurboTork Rayjay turbo-charger with big clearance forged Cosworth rally pistons fitted by Blydenstein.

The Silver Aero was used by GM in Germany for a while after the show, but it made its way back to the UK, and, although initially hard to track down, was sold through a Vauxhall dealer auction, eventually making its way into the hands of enthusiasts Mario and Edmund Lindsay, who also owned the Silver Bullet HC concept car described in the HC section of this book. At the time of writing, it has covered just 23,000 miles overall.

No van version of the Mk1 Cavalier was ever marketed. Although pick-up and enclosed panel van designs were studied in the styling studio, it was felt that the HA, Chevanne and later Astravan were covering the market well enough.

By the end of production over 230,000 Cavaliers had been produced, latterly in Luton, but with the coupé and Sports Hatch models imported.

Cavalier Mk1 media advertising slogans
Where family and sporty motoring come together
It performs like a race horse on roads designed for horse and carts
To keep your grip, you need more than the latest tyre technology
Funny how the competition rarely make comparisons
Isn't it time you fell in love with driving again? (GL)
Luxury that's hard to keep up with (GLS)
A smooth drive for the company man. An economy drive for the company
Turning heads comes as standard (coupé)
Your heart says one thing. Your head says another (coupé)
It'll make you want to take the long way home (coupé)
The Cavalier approach to the hatchback (Sports Hatch)
For Motorsport and Homes and Gardens (Sports Hatch)

CAVALIER Mk1 BODY TYPES: two- & four-door saloon, two-door coupé, two-door Sports Hatch, 1975-1981; **manufactured at**: Bochum (Germany), Antwerp (Belgium) and Luton (UK); **number produced**: 238,980.
PERFORMANCE: **top speed**: 87mph (142kph) (1300) to 111mph (182kph) (2-litre); **0-60mph (100kph)**: 9.2 sec (2-litre), 17.8 sec (1300); **average economy**: 23-30mpg.
PRICE AT LAUNCH: £2124.
MEASUREMENTS: **length**: 14ft 2in/4.3m (Sports Hatch) 14ft 7in/4.4m (coupé/saloon); **width**: 5ft 5in/1.65m; **height**: 4ft 6in (1.37m); **wheelbase**: 8ft 3in (2.52m); **weight**: 2005-2286lb (910-1037kg); **wheels**: 13in; **turning circle**: 31.1ft (9.47m); **fuel capacity**: 11 gallons (50 litres); **boot capacity**: 25ft^3 (saloon).
TECHNICAL: **engine types**: 1256, 1584, 1897, 1979cc four-cyl petrol; **gearbox**: four-speed manual, three-speed automatic (excl. 1300); **suspension**: independent front, coil springs, live axle coil spring at rear, brakes front disc, rear drum.
TRIM: vinyl, cloth, velour.
KEY OPTIONAL EXTRAS: automatic (not 1300), alloy wheels, metallic paint, sunroof, tow bar.

Cavalier Mk2

Enter the Cavalier Mk2 in late 1981: another badge-engineered Opel product, part of the worldwide J-car programme. Fuzzy pictures of the new J-car design had been published in the press as early as August 1980, depicting a two-door Ascona under cold Arctic weather testing. Initially in squarer-design four-door saloon and five-door hatchback forms only (the equivalent Opel Ascona 'C' could be bought with a two-door shell but some early Cavaliers 1300S two-doors made it through to production too), models came in the sporty two-tone painted SR then quickly SRi (1600), GLS (1600), GL (1300 and 1600), L (1300, 1600 and 1600 diesel) and base model (1300 and 1600). Like the Astra from the previous year, these were all front-wheel drive. An automatic option was made available on all models except the diesels, whilst manuals were four-speed on the 1300 and 1600s, with new five-speed on the 1600 GLS. This was true badge engineering: only trim changes and badging identified this as a Vauxhall rather than an Opel. A plush CD version joined the range in October 1982.

Rather alien to European eyes as far as Opel-badged cars were concerned, a rather practical five-door estate version was offered from October 1983, which was the only estate version produced on the three types of Cavalier (1975-1995). Unlike other previous Vauxhalls, the boot lid was almost vertical (as per contemporary Volvo estates), which gave rise to a cavernous 51ft^3 boot space with the 60/40 split rear seats folded down.

Cavalier Mk2 SR hatchback press advert.

A rear wash wipe system came as standard, and power was offered at only 1600cc. The low 18in loading height was attained by fixing the rear bumper to the bottom of the tailgate panel; for strength, retaining latches were fitted at base of each end of its opening. Both L and GL versions were available, and the estate continued production until the end of Mk2 production. The rearmost sections were imported from Holden in Australia, whose Camira J-Car formed the basis, and were delivered in CKD form, but sales were slower than expected given the availability of the slightly smaller Astra and slightly larger Carlton versions available alongside.

A Cavalier convertible was offered on the original, now deleted two-door platform from 1982. Rather tidy conversions were performed by Hammond and Theide, and were all-in 1800cc with Bosch fuel-injection form. Overall, around 118 were built (some sources state 1265), and two Opel Mantas were also converted by the Kent firm. Clever double page advertising stated: "Now we can promise you the moon," with a car depicted, roof down, under the stars at night, but apologies were offered that Vauxhall could not control the weather! Rear side glass could simply be wound down creating a superb panoramic effect (PA Cresta memories ...), and there were sports seats and front and rear spoilers.

Cavalier Mk2 CDi Mk2 saloon with caravan.

Despite the estate version selling slowly, the Mk2 Cavalier was a huge success. Indeed, it was Britain's best-selling car in 1984/85 when a quarter of a million cars were produced, seven-fold the 33,000 Cavaliers sold in 1981.

Essentially, the Mk2 shell went through

A two-tone Cavalier Mk2 SRi saloon.

The Cavalier Mk2 estate. Its rear panels were imported from Australia. The bumper was built into the tailgate and the load height was just 18.1in.

two face-lifts. The first was the 1985 model year, the most evident feature being the egg-crate front grille and larger headlamps and indicators. Automatic models now received a lower drive ratio resulting in better economy, there was new seating, and various previous options became standard, particularly on top-end models. The second face-lift occurred in 1987. Overall, these late model changes were well received, with numerous revisions including revised wheel covers, standardised rear seatbelts (their factory fitting was UK law by the following year), front grille, front bumper spoiler area and enhanced rear lamp treatment. Better trim was utilised inside, and a five-speed gearbox was standard across the range, apart from the base models. The 1.8-litre engine now utilised Low End Torque design for better performance and economy. The bigger 2-litre engine was introduced for the CD (now with Chain Velour trim), and the SRi adopted this engine a few months later (the SRi now fitted with Rally Twill trim along with the convertible, which also received a special colour co-ordinated rear boot spoiler). Central locking was now standard for the GL models upwards.

The SRi 130 (saloon/hatch) had the motoring hacks excited with its 119mph top speed and 0-60mph acceleration of 8.5 seconds (*Motor*), made possible by its 130PS engine and close ratio gearbox. It had special identifying decals, alloy wheels, front fog lights mounted with the spoiler and a large bore exhaust. *Motor* magazine also enthused that between 50-70mph in top gear "... will even out-haul the mighty M635 CSi."

Notable limited edition variants were the stylish Commander (saloon/hatch), the Antibes (1986 hatch), and the Club (saloon/hatch).

One particularly worthy limited edition was the 1987 Calibre saloon (note spelling) a smart Carmine Red car which still has quite a strong following, its name often misspelt for

A 1986 five-door hatch Cavalier Mk2.

The limited edition Cavalier Mk2 Calibre, now highly sought-after.

The Cavalier Mk2 convertible.

This convertible's interior has stood the test of time very well. Photographed summer 2022.

obvious reasons. Based on the more powerful SRi 130, the styling cues came from Tickford Aston Martin, and it featured full bodykit including side skirts, unique front and rear spoilers, Recaro seats etc. Sales were limited to 500 units, and an example was displayed on the 1987 UK Motor Show stand.

An eleventh hour, end of run limited edition, the attractive LX and 115mph LXi models came for February 1988, with a four-speaker digital stereo, sports steering wheel and instrumentation, lowered front spoiler and distinctive red stripe side mouldings. Alloy road wheels, sliding/tilting sunroof, close fitting Recaro style front seats and rear spoiler completed the look. In all, over 807,000 Mk2s were manufactured between 1981 and 1988: effectively one third of total Vauxhall sales to that date.

Cavalier Mk2 media advertising slogans

Refreshed. And not a drop of lager in sight
Top of the Class
You've read the facts. Now try the cars
Loaded with logic and acres of space (estate)
Punchy. Incredible load carrier (estate)
The family favourite
More dash, less cash (LX)
Even with kids he's still one of the boys
It takes more than stripes to make a Commander
Cavaliers, beware of Roundheads (SRi)
Endorsements will come as no surprise (SRi)
Plod no more (SRi)
It's nowhere near as far in the new SRi 130
You can see it on the back of the latest Cavaliers. If you're quick (injection)
This is the Year of the Cavalier. Again
Now it's our turn to be more generous with the Cavalier (GLSi)
More dash, less cash (face-lift)
It keeps on topping the league (face-lift)
Now we can promise you the moon (convertible)
Unzip a Cavalier (convertible)

BODY TYPES: two-door saloon, two-door convertible, four-door saloon, five-door hatch, five-door estate: 1981-1988; **manufactured at**: Luton; **number produced**: 807,624.
PERFORMANCE: (1600) **Top speed**: 106mph (174kph); **0-60mph (100kph)**: 12.5 sec; **average economy**: 30-35mpg (model dependant).
PRICE AT LAUNCH: £4820-£7389.
MEASUREMENTS: **length**: 14ft 4in/4.37m (saloon), 14ft 0in/4.27m (hatch), 14ft 2in/4.32m (estate); **width**: 5ft 6in/1.68m; **height**: 4ft 6½in (1.38m); **wheelbase**: 8ft 5½in (2.57m); **weight**: 2072-2491lb (940-1131kg); **wheels**: 13in; **turning circle**: 33.1 feet (10.1m); **fuel capacity**: 13.4 gallons (61 litre); **boot capacity**: 22.6ft^3 (saloon), 42.9ft^3 (hatch with seats down).
TECHNICAL: **engine types**: 1297, 1598, 1796, 1998cc four-cyl (petrol), 1598cc four-cyl (diesel); **gearbox**: four-speed & five-speed manual, three-speed automatic except diesel cars; **suspension**: independent MacPherson struts, coil springs (front), miniblock coil springs (rear); **brakes**: front disc, rear drum.
TRIM: cloth, velour.
KEY OPTIONAL EXTRAS: automatic transmission, central door locking, electric windows and aerial, metallic paint, power steering.

Cavalier Mk3

"Who says tomorrow never comes?" asked the first official advert title to the new third generation Cavalier in 1988. Here came, then, "The car of the future": an all-new sleek family car to replace the Mk2. The concept originated in 1982/83 with US designer Wayne Cherry and Project 2400, following fifth scale then full-size clay models in Russelsheim, the final tear drop design was frozen in early 1985 and the design specifics continued for another three years. The Mk2 Cavalier had certainly been a sales success, and the new Mk3 had a tough act to follow. Full-size prototypes were wind tested in Holland, Switzerland and Italy with a stunning resultant Cd factor of just 0.29.

A futuristic launch was proposed at the 1988 UK Motor Show. This tied in with 'The Car of the Future' TV advertising campaign, with the 1950s concept car built especially for the project making an appearance at the show, carefully shielded behind red roping alongside the new Cavaliers revolving on a

The Cavalier Mk3 saloon.

Press advert for the new 1988 Cavalier Mk3.

platform. The fake vehicle, very well finished, bore more than a passing resemblance to the US Lincoln Futura of 1955. The look was not initially complete: the nuclear 'family' in silver space-style suits was missing. On the first morning of the show, the girls arrived on schedule at 08:30, but the models' silver Lycra suits were three hours late, causing some

Interior of an early Cavalier Mk3 L.

embarrassment. Amongst the new line-up on show was a rally liveried 4x4 Cavalier.

The new car, launched at the same time as the near identical Opel Vectra, was available in two forms (four-door saloon, five-door hatch). For the Mk3 shape there was to be no estate model or any convertible type. Wayne Cherry's design team had cleverly made the saloon and hatch versions look almost identical from most angles, though beyond a cursory glance it could be seen that the rear-side glass of the hatch version was a little bigger. There were also to be novel four-wheel-drive versions, plus various top-end models. Model line-up was L, GL, SRi, and CD in four petrol engine versions: the new entry-level tax breaking 1.4-litre, the new Family 1 1.6-litre, the 2-litre (115hp and so called 'red top' 130hp 16v) plus a revised 1.7-litre diesel. The 4x4 and 135mph GSi were announced, but made available from early 1989. Anti-lock

The 1990 Cavalier Mk3 GSi 2000 4x4 16v. (Courtesy Lindon Lait)

The face-lifted Cavalier Mk3.

The Cesaro V6 Cavalier Mk3, in hatchback form.

Rear aspect of the V6 Cavalier Diplomat 2.5 24v Mk3 saloon.

brakes and automatic transmissions were the main options offered.

The 4x4 model, initially in L décor saloon only (the cheapest UK 2-litre 4x4 saloon was £11,750), drove the rear axle through a semi-viscous coupling. For added safety, it included an electronically controlled clutch pack that disconnected the rear drive under heavy braking. The £17,567 16v 4x4 GSi model had arrived, competing heavily against the dearer Sierra Sapphire Cosworth 4x4, plus the Peugeot 405 Mi 16x4 and Audi 90 quattro. Over 6000 4x4s were built.

Early 1992 saw the introduction of the completely different 1686cc Isuzu inspired 1.7-litre diesel now with turbo-charger, its better performance (up by 15mph top-end and a five-second reduction from 0-60mph) was noticeable around 2400rpm. The earlier, normally-aspirated diesel remained in production alongside.

By the end of 1992, a 1993 model year refresh occurred. This included a new body-coloured more rounded front grille with pronounced griffin logo, revised headlamps and front indicators, larger rear lamp clusters, revised wheel covers plus new alloy wheels. A Griffin badge was now placed in the centre of the boot lid. Non-visible improvements included the improvisation of twin side impact bars in each door, a body lock restraint system for the front seatbelts and extra sound insulation. The smallest 1.4-litre cars had vanished, but an Envoy 1.6-litre became the new entry level model. The Cavalier Turbo 4x4 had replaced the GSi 4x4, and the semi-sports SRi gained extra power. Turbocharging the 16v 2-litre engine increased power by a healthy 36 per cent. The factory stated that top speed was a dizzy 149mph through its six-speed gearbox (and good to see the speedo was calibrated to 160mph!), also seen in the top-line Calibra. 16in Turbine Blade alloy wheels completed the look with deeper front spoiler featuring integral fog lights, but, to its cost, fuel consumption was high in urban situations at around 23mpg.

The Cavalier Turbo 4x4 was listed as a new car until late 1994, bailing out at nearly £21,000, when the new 2-litre Ecotec engine replaced both existing 2-litre units. With specification close to the CD models, the new model year 1993 Cavalier V6 utilised four camshafts and four valves per cylinder, giving rise to a smoother 0-60mph of just over 9 seconds and a top speed of over 125mph. A five-speed manual and four-speed automatic was offered.

After some range rationalisation, the end of production range at July 1995 included the Envoy, LS, GLS, CDX and SRi, when the seven-year-old model was replaced by the new very similar-looking Vauxhall Vectra. The most expensive car at the time was the CDX 24v V6 five-door at £18,995. Sales, however, continued on run-out models for up to a year afterwards.

Various Mk3 Cavalier limited editions included: Concept (1991 and Concept II in 1994), Colorado (1993, and the only Cavalier with a CD player as standard fitment), Classic (1995), Expression (1991 then 1994-95), Cesaro (1993), Ethos (1993), Club (1994) and Diplomat (1992). Unlike many of the limited edition offerings of the early 1980s, these were factory produced vehicles that permanently gained a place in the new car listings in the weekly press price lists.

Cavalier Mk3 media advertising slogans

Who said tomorrow never comes?
Now it's crunch time for the competition
If we don't sell it, your Vauxhall doesn't need it
It's enough to make the Cavalier turn to 4-wheel-drive (4x4 L)
Striking performer, works hard, plays well
It's not a Cavalier, it's the Cavalier
The hard cell. The hard sell (Colorado)
In fuel economy tests, the Cavalier's nearest rival walked it (LS 1.6i)
Nice work if you can get it (GSi)
4x4=grip (4x4)
A great leap forward for turbos. One that doesn't (Turbo)
V Smooth, V Safe (V6)

BODY TYPES: four-door saloon, five-door hatch: 1988-1995; **manufactured at**: Luton; **number produced**: 862,000. Note 1,678,368 (Mk1, 2 & 3), last Mk3 built 21 July 1995.

PERFORMANCE: **top speed**: 94-149mph (154-245kph); **0-60mph (100kph)**: 20 sec (diesel), 6.4 sec (Turbo 4x4); **average economy**: 23-40mpg (all models).

Cavalier Mk3 SRi 16v on police duties.

PRICE AT LAUNCH: £7889 (1.4-litre).

MEASUREMENTS: **length**: 14ft 6½in/4.43m (saloon, 14ft 3¼in/4.35m (hatch); **width**: 5ft 7¼in (1.70m); **height**: 4ft 5in (1.39m); **wheelbase**: 8ft 6¼in (2.6m); **weight**: 2408-3083lb (1093-1399kg); **wheels**: 14/15in, plus 16in on Turbo; **turning circle**: 33.3- 34.8ft (10.1-10.6m); **fuel capacity**: 13.4/14.3 gallons (61/65 litres), standard/ sports models; **boot capacity**: 18.7ft³ except Turbo & 4x4 13.4ft³ (saloon), 16.2/45.5ft³ seats up/down (hatch).

TECHNICAL: **engine types**: 1389, 1598, 1998cc 8v, 1998 16v (all four-cyl, petrol), 2498cc (six-cyl, petrol), 1699/1686cc four-cyl, diesels); **gearbox**: five-speed on all except six-speed Turbo 4x4, automatic four-speed optional; **suspension**: independent MacPherson struts with coil springs at front, progressive rate minibloc coil springs (4x4 & Turbo are independent at rear); **brakes**: front disc, rear drum (disc on larger-engined cars).

TRIM: cloth, velour, leather.

KEY OPTIONAL EXTRAS: automatic transmission, roof rack, tow bar, spoilers, darkened rear lights, Sportstyle styling.

Calibra

A year after the new Cavalier Mk3 was first displayed, pre-production prototypes of the Calibra coupé were displayed at the 1989 UK Motor Show alongside the Lotus Carlton. It received the *Autocar & Motor* award for best car design that year. Production was some time off. The emphasis at the show was on the Calibra's sleek lines and

An early UK 'G' registered Calibra press car.

A Calibra SE2 limited edition.

Incredibly, the Calibra 4x4 Turbo was Towcar of the Year in 1993.

Centre dashboard of the Calibra.

aerodynamics, and it was now officially the most aerodynamic car on the planet. The 8v model had a stunning Cd factor of 0.26, with the 16v having 0.28 due to wider tyres and other minor differences.

Manufactured in Russelsheim, the first dealer demonstration Calibras quietly arrived on the docks at the Isle of Sheppey, 42 miles east of central London, in May 1990. These wore the UK 'G' registration prefix, and were soon making their way to keen motoring journalists who felt that, with their rigorous testing and much wheel-spinning activities, the new car would benefit from four-wheel-drive and air-conditioning ...

The car soon became available for sale, and that four-wheel-drive was made into a production model shortly after. In 1992, a 4x4 Turbo was announced, complete with six-speed Getrag gearbox offering startling mid-range acceleration and top speed a shade over 150mph. Over its seven-year production run, the complete Calibra range included: 2.0 8v, 2.0 16v, 2.0 16v 4x4, SE1 (8v), SE2 (16v), SE3 (8v), SE4 (8v), SE5 (8v), SE6 (8v), SE7 (16v), SE8 (16v), SE9 (V6), Tickford Calibra, Turbo (1992) and Turbo DTM, with engines coming from contemporary Cavaliers. Perhaps the most memorable was the DTM with striking yellow flashes on its white bodywork. The Calibra's main rivals were the less powerful (and less successful) Ford Probe and VW Corrado. Valmet Automotive built two Calibra cabriolet examples, but officially GM only produced the three-door coupé also badged as Chevrolet and Holden across the world.

A major face-lift occurred in 1994 when,

The Calibra Turbo 4x4.

The 1993 Calibra V6 shared the Cavalier engine.

just like on the Mk3 Cavaliers, a Griffin badge appeared in the centre of the boot panel, plus a revised corporate V-style front grille with 'Griffin' central, rather than the previously bonnet-mounted example. The distinctive ultra thin headlamp units remained.

From late 1991, before the SE1-SE9 series of cars had been introduced, 26 Tickford Calibras were built. The SE series consisted of all individual cars, often in their own bespoke colour schemes. A limited edition Keke Rosberg Calibra was produced for the continental market, whilst the final run-out Turbo Limited Edition was made in jet black, was lower by 35mm, and had an Irmscher spoiler and stylish BBS alloy wheels.

The model was not built from June 1997, but there were some UK registrations appearing after this date. At time of writing there are around 1900 Calibras stated as SORN (not taxed and off the road), and 400 taxed and still on UK roads.

Leather seating for the V6 and Turbo models.

The Calibra Turbo limited edition.

A Calibra DTM in replicated racing colours.

Calibra media advertising slogans

Enter desire (4x4)
Vauxhall's stunning new start to the nineties
The difference £15 can make to a high-performance Vauxhall
In most £17,000 cars, leather is the thing you use to mop the windows (SE4)
The performance. The best seats
Warning. It's photogenic (SE)
1st 1st 1st (Calibra, & 24v/Lotus Carlton)

BODY TYPES: three-door coupé: 1989-1997; **manufactured at**: Russelsheim (Germany) & Uusikaupunki (Finland); **number produced**: 40,460.

PERFORMANCE: **top speed**: 124-152mph (203-250 kph); **0-60mph**: 10 sec-6.4 sec (8v auto & Turbo 4x4 compared); **average economy**: 25-32mpg.

PRICE AT LAUNCH: £14,750 (2.0i).

MEASUREMENTS: **length**: 14ft 9in (4.5m); **width**: 5ft 6½in (1.69m); **height**: 4ft 4in (1.32m); **wheelbase**: 8ft 6in (2.6m); **weight**: 2675-2912lb (1214-1324kg); **wheels**: 15in, 16in on 4x4 Turbo; **turning circle**: 34.8ft (10.6m); **fuel capacity**: 14 gallons (63 litres); **boot capacity**: 10.6/34.6ft^3 (seats up/down).

TECHNICAL: **engine types**: 1998cc four-cyl & 2498cc (V6) petrol; **gearbox**: 5- & six-speed manual, four-speed automatic; **suspension**: MacPherson struts and independent coil springs at front, independent rear with miniblock springs; **brakes**: disc all round.

TRIM: cloth, velour, leather.

KEY OPTIONAL EXTRAS: AF20 automatic transmission, uprated wheels, ski racks, Sportstyle bodykit, velour mats.

Dashboard of the 1996 Calibra V6. Note its white instrument dials.

The 16v engine as fitted to the Calibra.

Interior of the Tickford Calibra.

The Calibra SE6 of 1996.

Front-wheel drive arrives: Astra Mk1, 2 and 3

Astra Mk1

By 1980, the Vauxhall range consisted of four mainstream models: the V-car Carlton/ Royales, the Chevettes, and the original rear-wheel drive Cavalier Mk1s. Enter the wedge-shaped Astra Mk1, styled with a deep air dam at the front, high tail at the rear and flowing body lines.

The new T-car was first seen by the public in September 1979, by way of the near-identical Opel Kadett 'D', aimed at competing with the Fiat Ritmo (Strada in UK), VW Golf, Talbot Horizon and forthcoming Ford Escort Mk3. The new generation of German-built front-wheel drive Vauxhalls hit the sales floors the following spring and instantly became a hit with the buying public, in fleet, hire and private sectors. Originally offered in a confusing line-up opposite its Opel Kadett cousin, only two versions were available: the Astra 1300 GL five-door saloon (a £4601 hatch) and a £4324 1300 L estate (50ft^3 with seats down). It sat nicely between the dearer Cavalier and cheaper Chevette ranges, replacing the now

The new Astra Mk1 two-door of 1980.

Dashboard of the new Astra.

Original Astra five-door estate.

The first Astra off the Ellesmere production line in 1981.

somewhat ageing HC Viva/Magnums that had seen a nine-year production run.

Styling was from Germany, under Director of Design Henry Haga. "It's what the roads have been waiting for ..." hailed the press adverts in early 1980, boasting of exceptional stability at speed and in cross winds. A world first for under 1500cc: hydraulic valve lifters, 98mph and 0-60mph in a shade over 12 seconds. The economy, particularly at speed, knocked spots off the competition. The prototypes were subjected to wind tunnel testing in Pininfarina's facility in Turin, with a commendable (for the small size) Cd figure of 0.39 attained, when most cars of the time were still around 0.45. Worthy of note was the small roof spoiler built in at the rear.

The 1.2-litre and 1.3-litre Opel Kadett were marketed as an extensive range including two-door (booted), three-door and the regular five-door saloon and estate (and sports 1.3 SR), and it was not long until the new Vauxhall Astra range was offered in the UK. The first 1980 brochures listed the 1300 engine only, but, very soon, the (quite rare booted, but same shape and length) 1200S three-door (£3404) or five-door versions, identified by their round headlamps and black surrounds, were marketed as the Astra Saloon. Alongside these small, old, Opel overhead valve-engined Astras, the new 1300S was offered in three- and five-door hatch plus estate derivatives. Then, for the 1982 model year, a new 1.6-litre engine became available for the better trimmed models.

In November 1981, Astra Mk1 production was moved to Ellesmere Port in the UK, thus away from the GM Bochum plant, and the German-built two-door booted Astra was quietly discontinued. A booted Mk1 Astra was a rare sight, usually bought by the fleet and car hire sector, and identified from the rear by two large and rather ugly black hinge covers, just on the top edge of the boot line. The author worked with a colleague in the early 1980s who had bought one from new. His appraisal was that his small excited poodle could not jump out of the rear each time the boot was opened!

1.6-litre diesel-engined variants were available from mid-1982 in both saloon and estate bodyshells, with a new engine also used in the Cavalier Mk2. Further trim derivatives were the L décor and base models, too.

The first sporting factory-built Astra was announced in September 1982. This was

The Astra SR had its lower section in black.

The Astra GTE in the Vauxhall heritage collection.

the Astra 1600S SR, a three-door hatch with two-tone paint, windscreen shade-band, front dam spoiler, larger rear roof spoiler, alloy wheels with low profile radial tyres, headlamp pressure washers and a five-speed gearbox. To enhance the sporty image, the GL's Chevron tweed cloth trim was extended to Recaro seats in the front.

The SR was followed under a year later by the 115hp Astra GTE three-door hatch, an even 'hotter' car, this time with the 1.8-litre Bosch fuel-injected engine seen in the Cavalier SRi and Opel Manta and revised Carltons, albeit in less cooked form. Costing £6412, (£600 more than the SR), the GTE boasted Chicago velour trim front and rear with white piping, Recaro front seats, all the styling attributes of the SR plus new running boards, as well as the restrained, extrovert, full colour co-ordinated Polar White offering. Unlike the SR, this model saw the introduction of an angular rear spoiler below the back bumper that incorporated twin high-intensity fog lamps. Also a first for this bodyshell were wheelarch extensions. It competed head-on with the shorter wheelbase Golf GTi and Escort XR3i, with the Vauxhall media copywriters claiming it was "Built to make your heart beat faster ..."

Another popular advert of the time claimed "Nought to naughty naughty in 8.5 seconds," with a rear shot of a white car turning into

Press advertising with a teaser regarding its rapid acceleration, where legal!

The Astra EXP limited edition with gold steel wheels.

The original Bedford Astravan.

a fast twisty B road on the moors. Later advertising included strong references to the Brian Wiggins racing Astra GTE. For clarity there was an SRi which made its debut in August 1986.

Before Astra Mk1 production ceased, other editions of the Mk1 included the limited edition 1982 two-tone £4995 EXP and EXP S (offered with gold wheels), and the 1984 Celebrity five-door hatch. One beefed-up vehicle was the 72hp 102mph Blydenstein Turbo conversion to the 1300 for an extra £1000. There was the (enclosed-only) Bedford Astravan, a van version for the 1983 model year. This took over where the Chevanne had left off, and yet still sold alongside the somewhat cheaper and now ageing HA Viva van.

Mk1 Astra media advertising slogans

It's what roads have been waiting for
Loads better, pace setter (estate)
Exclusive. Inclusive (EXP)
Built to make your heart beat faster (GTE)
Naught to naughty naughty in 8.5 seconds (GTE)
Dealership to championship in one quick gear change (GTE)

ASTRA Mk1 BODY TYPES: three-door & five-door hatch, five-door estate: 1980-1984; **manufactured at**: Ellesmere Port; **number produced**: 1,117,662 incl Mk2.
PERFORMANCE: **top speed**: 115mph (188kph); **0-60mph (100kph)**: 9.5 sec (1.8 GTE); **average economy**: 30-40mpg.
PRICE AT LAUNCH: £3404 (**two-door**).
MEASUREMENTS: **length**: 13ft 1½in/4.0m (hatch), 13ft 9½in/4.21m (estate); **width**: 5ft 4½in (1.64m); **height**: 4ft 4¼in/1.33m (hatch), 4ft 5in/1.34m (estate); **wheelbase**: 8ft 3in (2.51m); **weight**: 1852-2238lb (840-1015kg); **wheels**: 13in (SR & GTE 14in); **turning circle**: 32.6ft (9.9m); **fuel capacity**: 9.2 gallons/42 litres (hatch), 11 gallons/50 litres (estate); **boot capacity**: 10.3/50ft^3 (hatch/estate).
TECHNICAL: **engine types**: 1196, 1297, 1598, 1796cc petrol four-cyl, petrol plus 1598cc four-cyl diesel; **gearbox**: four-speed & five-speed (SR & GTE) manual plus three-speed automatic option; **suspension**: independent MacPherson struts, coil springs (front), miniblock coil springs (rear); **brakes**: front disc, rear drum.
TRIM: cloth, velour, Recaro front in SR and GTE.
KEY OPTIONAL EXTRAS: rear seatbelts, sunroof, metallic paint, alloy wheels, five-speed manual & automatic transmission.

Astra Mk2

A radical change to Vauxhall's small mid-sized car was first seen in September 1984 by way of the Mk2 Astra, almost identical to its German cousin, the Kadett type E, code-named T-85 by GM. Again built in Ellesmere Port after a £50 million investment in robotics, from its inception there were quite a few models in the range, utilising the familiar running gear from the Mk1s, with 1.2-, 1.3-, 1.6- and 1.8-litre engines, plus again a 1.6-litre diesel. Three- and five-door hatches plus an estate (and the Bedford Astravan) were marketed. Unlike the Mk1, estates were now sold as both three-door and five-door, the bottom line three-door being 20kg lighter with fewer trim options.

The new Astra Mk2 Merit.

The Astra Mk2 Merit interior.

Top of the range was the 1.8-litre GTE three-door with colour-coded bumpers and mirror, later joined, curiously and briefly, by a five-door GTE (sold August 1985 to early 1987). The new model's slippery shape, helped along by bonded front and rear screens and rear wheelarches that partly covered the wheels, was way more aerodynamic, with a Cd factor of 0.30 for the tail-planed GTE – a record-breaking figure only just reached by the larger Audi 100 two years previously. Overall fuel consumption was reduced by about 6 per cent. The GTE secured a commendable 126mph, its large rear spoiler helping reduce drag by up to 25 per cent. The Astra GTE utilised the LCD instrumentation originally seen in the Monza GSE and Senators. All models had the same wheelbase as the Mk1 version at 99.2in, although they were very slightly wider and taller. Flush fitting wheel covers were the order of the day with 14in alloys an optional extra.

Various limited editions commenced from 1986 through to 1990. Antibes, Shadow, Diamond, Jubilee, Swing, Tiffany, Eclipse, Starlight and Starmist to name a few.

A new 16-valve 2-litre engine was sold with top line GTEs from spring 1987. With 150hp, there was a claimed 138mph top speed and 0-60mph time of 7.3 seconds. Improvements were made to the braking system and the ride height was further lowered. Apart from the 16v badging, identification at the rear was easy: the new hot hatch had twin rectangular exhausts. Interestingly, this was described as a two-door car in the sales catalogues.

Announcing in January 1986 "A more elegant way to travel," the range was complimented with a new booted version, the Belmont four-door saloon, offering a bigger boot at 19ft^3 and a 60/40 split folding seat arrangement. The Belmont was some 9in longer than the hatch; almost entirely matching the estate versions, its extra length was all behind the rear wheels. Belmont to Astra could be compared with Ford Orion to Escort. Although no sports Belmont was offered at first (just the 1800 GLSi), a sporty 121mph Belmont SRi headed the range for the 1987 model year, and there was soon a red Belmont Jubilee limited edition joining the hatch and estate Jubilee versions, all with plaid upholstery, tinted glass, sports wheels, stereo radio-cassette and four speakers. By Motor Show time, entry level models across the board were joined by the Astra Merit.

In early 1987, around 'D' registration time

Rear aspect of the four-door Astra Swing hatchback.

At £15,800, the 1993 Mk2 Astra Exclusive convertible was the most expensive Mk2 Astra produced.

for the UK, the 2.0 GTE Astra convertible was marketed. This had a strengthened bulkhead and sills, its roof opened and closed at the touch of a button, and it was styled and built by Bertone in Italy. The marketing hype was quick to point out that GTE stood for "Great Tan Expected"! This was quickly followed by a 1.6-litre cabriolet within a few months. The 1990 model year saw colour co-ordinated hoods on the Pearl Red and Pearl Blue cars. 6764 convertibles were reported built, and these continued until 1993 with the Mk2 shell, well after Mk2 production ceased.

An interesting advertisement appeared in November 1992 depicting an Astra convertible with a Lamborghini Muira, Ferrari Dino GT4 and Maserati Khamsin on a stunning Italian hillside, the copy boasting about the virtues of having Nuccio Bertone as a designer.

In spring 1987, the Club Astra was only available as a 1.3-litre five-door hatch to mirror the Club Cavalier and Club Nova of the

A 1990 Mk2 Astra L estate.

The four-door Belmont saloon in sporty SRi guise seen on Felixstowe seafront. When new it was £10,576

time (there was a 1.3-litre Club Belmont, too). These limited editions came in white only, with unique grey/yellow seating, grey carpets, door and boot badging, low profile tyres and tinted glass. White bumpers with black inserts and white wheel covers finished the effect.

From late 1989, and alongside the 124PS 2-litre GTE, a 135mph 150PS double overhead camshaft 16v version was sold, costing an extra £1600 over the standard GTE, with twin anti-roll bars and revised suspension setup, resulting in the car sitting 10mm lower

The SRi had these attractive door decals.

to the ground. Identified by red 16v emblems under the rear GTE badging and on the nearside front spoiler, these sought-after 16v versions were fitted with a leathered-covered three-spoke steering wheel, and this rapid car had an integral three-way catalytic converter. Under the bonnet, a further 16v reminder was a red panel on the rocker box cover with "VAUXHALL DOHC 16v" stamped on it (this became known affectionately as the 'red-top' engine). At the rear were dual rectangular tailpipes, reminding following traffic this was the hottest Astra. Whilst the gear ratios were identical, to avoid over-revving at top speeds, the final drive ratio was brought down from 3.43:1 to 3.33:1.

To commemorate its 25-year anniversary at the Ellesmere Port factory, Vauxhall embarked on a styling exercise based on a Mk2 GTE dubbed Quicksilver. Registered E690YVS, this March 1988 registered vehicle was displayed at the Birmingham Motor Show as a one-off design concept. It remained unused for many years afterwards; an MoT in 2008 reveals it failing on many of the perishable parts after just 57 miles driven. At the time of writing it still has only 5000 miles on the clock, having passed each of its subsequent MoT tests on the first attempt. It had a unique blended silver body and full leather interior.

By early 1989 a face-lift was performed. Models had a revised front grille, bumper and badge treatment, whilst new wheel covers brightened up the side aspect. A new top trim CD model became available with power steering, central locking and wood door cappings on the saloon and hatch platforms, "The new Astra CD, rather more gear than the Ghia," stated the adverts – a direct comparison to the Ford Escort 1.6 Ghias of the time. Rome velour interior trim completed the executive look. Belmonts now became Astra Belmonts.

In the 1989 model year, the attractively trimmed Astra Belmont LXi estate could outrun the competition with a 0-60mph time of 9.5 seconds. A run out limited edition in summer 1990 with standard sunroof came in three- and five-door, in Glacier White or Flame Red. This was the Starlight, starting at £7546. The new 1.7-litre diesel was offered in the 1989 model year, with power up from 54 to 57PS.

The entry level Belmont saloon, initially available with 1.3-, 1.6- and 1.8-litre petrol engines, plus a 1.6-litre diesel engine.

The attractive Belmont LXi estate seating.

Vauxhall heritage collection Astra GTE 16v Mk2.

The GTE interior with the AC Delco digital LCD dashboard.

More press advertising depicting top speed, the Astra GTE Mk2.

From the spring of 1990, a 'Leather Edition' limited edition 16v GTE Astra was offered. Around 250 examples were sold from London dealers, with pearlescent red Bordeaux paint, Connolly leather door cards, Recaro seats, uprated DC681 hi-fi sound system, special catalytic converter, ABS and cross-spoked alloy wheels with low profile tyres. To further identify them away from mainstream models, there was a small three colour flash on the tailgate and rear body sides, in GM racing colours. The advert headlines read "Hide & Sleek."

Into 1991, and further late model Mk2 Astras included the Astra LX, LXi, GL, SX and SXi, in hatch and estate form, these sporty cars had alloy wheels, front fog lamps, tinted glass and small rear spoiler. Unlike the previous SRi, body colour was identical under the waist band. As an anecdote, the two most stolen cars in a 2005 survey were the Mk2 Astra and Belmont, with one in thirteen Belmonts stolen throughout their life.

The Bedford Astravan was basically the same size as the estate, whilst the Astramax van enjoyed an extended curved roof line for extra capacity, with twin vertical rear doors and a carrying capacity of 635kg.

Mk2 Astra media advertising slogans

He who hesitates has lost

Vauxhall announce a more elegant way to travel. Belmont class

Travel Belmont class. We never forget you have a choice (Belmont)

If we don't sell it, your Vauxhall doesn't need it (Belmont)

Which is the business end? (Belmont LXi estate)

You'll be surprised what the new Belmont SRi can take on

The car for the 90s (convertible)

When you're buying a sporty car, it's nice to know the designer's had a bit of practice (convertible)

Astravan and Astramax Bedford light vans on the Mk2 platform.

An expression of delight. An expression of relief (Expression)
You can now get 14 Rovers in the back of an Astra (estate)
Now you can see how we got there first (GTE)
Around town we recommend the 4-seater version (GTE)
Top of its year as well as top of its class (GTE)
Fly on the wall (GTE)
Since time has began man has wanted to fly (GTE)
Try this simple aerodynamic test on your car (GTE)
... fastest in its class thanks to a 4000hp engine (GTE)
Hide & sleek (GTE 16v Leather Edition)
The 1987 Astras. Now with 17 gear changes
The superior Astra range. We've even given it a nose to look down
Heart stopping (and no, that's not the price) (SXi)
The Astra 16v so reliable we called out the RAC
For the perfect town car, just add water (SRi)
Rather more gear than a Ghia (CD)
Free with the Astra Starlight. Sunlight

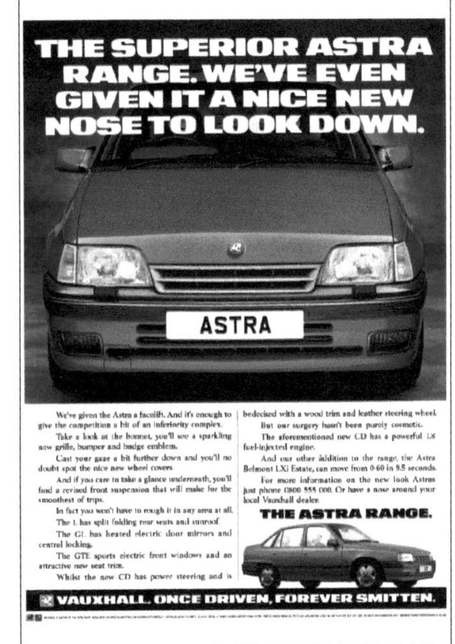

The revised front end of the face-lifted Astra Mk2.

ASTRA Mk2 BODY TYPES: three-door & five-door hatch, five-door estate, four-door saloon, cabriolet, van: 1984-1991; **manufactured at**: Ellesmere Port; **number produced**: 1,117,662 incl Mk1.

PERFORMANCE: **top speed**: 96-135mph (158-235kph)**; 0-60mph (100kph)**: GTE 16v: 8.0 sec; **average economy**: 28-42mpg model dependant.

PRICE AT LAUNCH: £4494 (1.2S).

MEASUREMENTS: **length**: 13ft 1½in/3.99m (hatch & cabrio), 13ft 10in/4.22m (Belmont), 11ft 10½in/4.23m (estate); **width**: 5ft 5½in (1.66m); **height**: 4ft 7in/1.39m (hatch & Belmont), 4ft 8½in/1.43m (estate), 4ft 6½in/1.38m (cabriolet), 5ft 5½in/1.67m (Astramax van); **wheelbase**: 8ft 3in (2.52m); **weight**: 1851-2248lb (840-1010kg);

wheels: 13in, SR/SRi & GTE 14in; **turning circle**: 32.2ft (9.8m); **fuel capacity**: 11.4 gallons/52 litres (hatch), 11 gallons/50 litres (estate); **boot capacity**: 14/53ft^3 (hatch/estate).
TECHNICAL: **engine types**: 1196, 1297, 1389, 1598, 1796, 1998cc petrol four-cyl petrol plus 1598cc & 1700cc four-cyl diesel; **gearbox**: four-speed & five-speed (SR & GTE) manual plus three-speed automatic option; **suspension**: independent MacPherson struts, coil springs (front), miniblock coil springs (rear); **brakes**: front disc, rear drum.
TRIM: cloth, velour, Recaro front in SR and GTE.
KEY OPTIONAL EXTRAS: rear seatbelts, sunroof, metallic paint, alloy wheels, five-speed manual & automatic transmission.

Astra Mk3

Just ahead of the 1991 UK Motor Show, the new Mk3 Vauxhall Astra made its debut. Twenty-second teaser adverts were shown on TV after extensive filming in July. Once again based on the Opel platform, this time the Germans took their new model name from the UK cars, and thus the Opel Astra was born on the continent.

Gone was the name Belmont. The new line-up consisted of four-door saloon, five-door estate, three- and five-door hatch models, plus the estate shaped van. Powertrains available were Family 2 (new) 1.4- and 1.6-litre petrol engines, plus a 1.7-litre diesel. These came in various trim guises, including Merit, L, LS, GLS, Duo, CD, CDX and Si. Sports models were again 2-litre, in SRi and top specification GSi form. Vauxhall marketing in 1991 stated it was "Every car you'll ever need" on double page press adverts. For middle management there was a 2.0 CD. A 2.0-litre SRi estate was also marketed. Alloy road wheels were standard on the CD and GSi cars.

All petrol models were now fuel injected. *Autocar & Motor* magazine enthused "... the better-looking new Astra leaves most of its rivals for dead when it comes to refinement, build quality and economy." Thus the new Astra utilised the old model's engines and floorpans, very strong features of the previous car, but were clothed in a roomier, glassier, stiffer and more aerodynamic body. Coupled with new interior and sweepier dashboards, the new car brought the small to mid-sized car into the 1990s, and it sold very well.

"Fancy taking it for a spin? Well you can't" were the advert headlines for the new GSi, which now had ETC (Electronic Traction Control) engineered mainly to cope with slippery surfaces. Autumn 1993 saw some subtle changes to the chassis of the GSi, following press reports that the handling was not as good as it could have been. Fine

An early Astra Mk3 CD.

The Astra Mk3 Diamond estate.

tuning of the existing parts couple with harder suspension bushes seemed to cure the issues. Spring rates were reduced and the tyres reduced from 205/50 to 195/60 14s.

Initially the Astra convertible continued using the Mk2 shell (echoes of the Mk1 VW Golf cabriolet idea), and, despite the press leaking pictures as early as August 1991, the 2-litre Astra convertible based on a revised Mk3 shell was marketed from June 1993. It was dubbed "Britain's coolest tanning machine" on the press adverts towards the end of that year. By April 1994, two open-roof models were available: the 1.6-litre with a manually operated roof, and the better specification manual-only 1.8-litre with power-operated roof and improved radio. This car was strictly four seats only. There was a considerable £2750 price difference, and the larger-engined car could beat its stable-mate by a creditable 3½ seconds on the 0-60mph tests (10 seconds versus 13.5). The sporty Cesaro appeared early in 1994, just pre-face-lift.

In the summer of 1994 the Astra went through a face-lift, with new engines, improved suspension, and power steering standardised (with fewer turns lock to lock). By now the sporty 150bhp GSi was discontinued, although this was back yet again in revised form before the Astra Mk3 was discontinued in 1998. These new 1995 season models were identified by an Omega-inspired V grille, white indicators, slimmer headlamps and side rubbers. The hatch and the saloon now shared the same revised rear lamps. Interiors had softer seats and door trims, plus better carpets, and for the driver there was a wide-angle door mirror.

Astra Mk3 16v GSi in cutaway form.

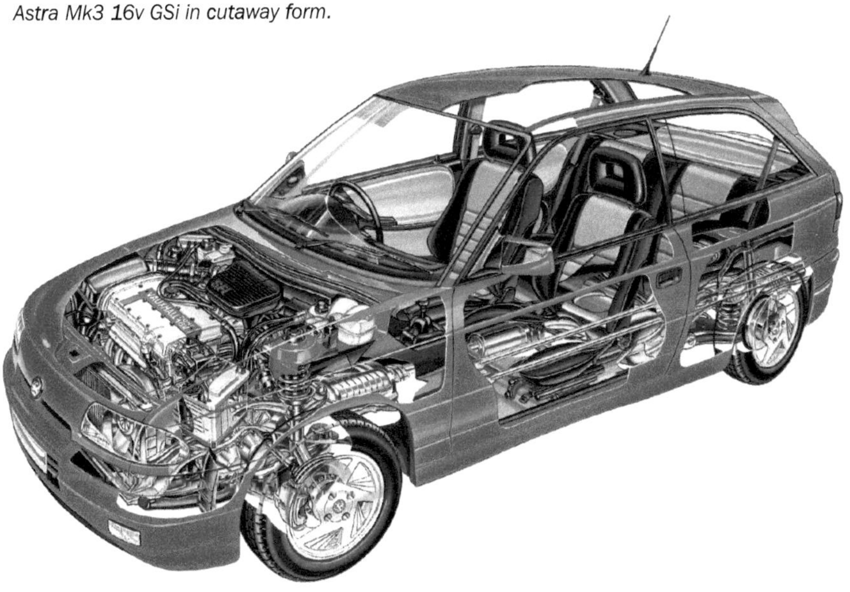

Electronic Traction Control forms the basis for this press advert on the Astra GSi.

Ironically this Vauxhall was one of the most stolen car types in the UK in the 1990s.

£16,278 bought you this Mk3 Astra convertible.

The Belmont name was dropped for the Astra Mk3 saloon shell.

Engines offered at this point were the 1.6i, 1.8i and the 60hp 1.7-litre diesel, which was no longer normally-aspirated but was of light pressure type (up to 67hp), decreasing the DERV-powered car's 0-60mph time by over 2 seconds to 14.5. The revised 36-strong range was now: base model Merit, LS, GLS and Sport, plus the convertible. All engines could be ordered with Sport specification, with larger wheels and deep body-coloured bumpers to identify. All manual models were five-speeders, the Sport models with close ratios. With no GSi version at this point, the Sport held the chequered flag with its unique Wave cloth seat trim and body-coloured rear roof spoiler on the hatch version. The largest petrol-engined car also featured ABS braking, eight-spoke alloy wheels, rev counter and Driver Information Centre on the dash.

The top executive CDX soon followed with air-conditioning on petrol versions. It was now the only Astra model to feature the ECOTEC 136PS 2-litre 16v engine in top specification form, although the engine was used in final production year in the 1997 reintroduced GSi, again with the lower-powered Ecotec engine and a slightly altered bodykit (the rear spoiler was longer and had an integrated brakelight). Bonnet vents were gone, but there were fluted side skirts and less pronounced badging.

Vauxhall produced a leaflet in December 1996 detailing a new GSi. This less powerful (and thus cheaper to insure) model finally made it into reviewers' hands by July 1997, with last minute suspension modifications following consultation with Lotus. Vauxhall stated this 2.0i 16v model was not a replacement for the earlier GSi – more of an enhancement to the Sport models.

Before the end of Mk3 production, there were several tempting options offered via the factory, including Vauxhall I-Line and Irmscher

Official Astra Line accessories fitted to this Mk3 saloon.

styling to individualise cars: revised spoilers, uprated coil springs, a 2-litre performance kit and Chromestar-Design alloy wheels that had more than a passing resemblance to the Lotus Carlton. There was even a matching rear lower spoiler for the Astra convertibles (now 1.6- and 1.8-litre) that matched the front air dam.

By 1998, the Mk3 had disappeared from the price lists, making way for the new bigger Mk4. There had been various limited edition models throughout its seven-year production run, including: Expression, Artic, Artic 2, California, Arizona, Premier, Cesaro, Montana, Diamond, Swing, Ethos, Pacific and Atlas. Sadly the Lotus, V6 and four-wheel-drive versions that were rumoured pre-launch in 1991, never made it to fruition.

Mk3 Astra media advertising slogans

The new Astra from Vauxhall. We thought we'd ring the changes

Vauxhall now produce every car you'll ever need

So you find seatbelts boring? Here's one that'll really grab you

Even the car is wearing a safety belt

Heat seeking (convertible)

Britain's coolest tanning machine (convertible)

Fancy taking it for a spin? Well you can't (GSi)

So well behaved, you won't even hear a squeak from the tyres (GSi)

Every car you'll ever need. And more to boot (saloon)

Vauxhall introduces the world's least portable radio

Drive the new Astra and help change the face of cycling

79,800 square centimetres of California, £9570 (California)

The Astra Club. Exclusive membership £11,280 (Club estate)

The Mk3 Astravan. There was no Astramax high-roof Mk3; the Mk2 continued until the Corsa-inspired Combo van was introduced.

ASTRA Mk3 BODY TYPES: three-door & five-door hatch, five-door estate, four-door saloon, cabriolet, van: 1991-1998; **manufactured at**: Ellesmere Port; **number produced**: 606,350.

PERFORMANCE: **top speed**: 121mph (199kph) (GSi); **0-60mph (100kph)**: 9.5 sec; **average economy**: 30-44mpg model dependant.

PRICE AT LAUNCH: £10,201.

MEASUREMENTS: **length**: 13ft 1in (3.99m) (cabrio), 13ft 3in (4.04m) (hatch), 13ft 10in (4.21m) (saloon), 14ft 0in (4.27m) (estate); **width**: 5ft 6½in (1.69m); **height**: 4ft 6¼in/1.38m (cabrio) 4ft 7½in/1.41m (hatch & saloon) 4ft 10in (1.48m) (estate); **wheelbase**: 8ft 3in (2.52m); **weight**: 2104-2607lb (955-1183kg); **wheels**: 14in (13in on Merit & LS); **turning circle**: 32.2ft (9.8m); **fuel capacity**: 11.4 gallons/52 litres (hatch), 11 gallons/50 litres (estate); **boot capacity**: 12.7/57.6ft^3 (hatch & estate with seat down).

TECHNICAL: **engine types**: 1389, 1598, 1998cc petrol four-cyl petrol plus 1686cc four-cyl diesel; **gearbox**: five-speed manual, four-speed automatic; **suspension**: independent MacPherson struts, coil springs (front), miniblock coil springs (rear); **brakes**: front disc, rear drum.

TRIM: cloth, velour, leather.

KEY OPTIONAL EXTRAS: automatic gearbox, air-conditioning, uprated sound system, ABS, rear levelling system (estate), metallic paint, spoilers and other bodykit.

Later small cars: Nova, Corsa and Tigra

Nova

Six months after the continental launch of the Opel Corsa 'A', Vauxhall introduced the Nova, essentially a mildly anglicised version of the Corsa, in April 1983. This was to gradually replace the rear-wheel-drive Chevette that remained in production for a few more months albeit in reduced range form, sales of which were already affected by the 1980 Astra.

Both a three-door hatch and a two-door saloon were available at launch. Unique in the range, the hatch model had distinctive flared wheelarches (akin to the Audi Quattro of the day), and, unlike the Chevette, there was no estate version available. The booted version gave an extra 8ft^3 of storage capacity, gained by the extra 13in in overall length, all found after the rear wheels. Road wheels were 13in, the larger 14in only specified on the SR, which could be ordered with alloys – a sensible choice.

From the outset, the specification range consisted of base model, L and SR, the latter being the 1.3-litre sportier version with two-tone coachwork and in three-door form only to match its racing cousins. Lesser models came in 1-litre and 1.2-litre petrol only, the bigger 1.5-litre turbo diesel not arriving until November 1989 and the 1.6-litre GTE in 1988.

Following a concept car shown at the 1984 UK Motor Show, in January 1985 the Nova Sport, a homologation special, was created so Vauxhall could compete in sports events against heavy competition. Just 502 examples were produced with the input of Steve Thompson Cars (Opel and Irmscher specialist). These were based on the standard three-door shell, always in white with racing colour graphics and a five-speed gearbox. Cars were delivered in SR form with six-dial clocks and Recaro interior from Spain, and the Irmscher kit could be added by mechanics at the main dealer. The 1.3-litre engine's camshaft was uprated from 75 to 93hp to bring down the 0-60mph acceleration time by a commendable two seconds; quicker than the standard SR with carburettor changes, too. Whilst some of these cars have had a hard life

The original Nova two-door saloon.

The original SR Nova, always in hatch form. Steel wheels were standard fitting.

The Nova Swing limited edition three-door hatchback.

and vanished, they still have quite a following.

A GL version had joined the line-up by 1984 along with a more basic Merit by 1986, and for the 1987 model year a very neat (for a small car) four-door saloon was added. Five-door hatches were now sold, albeit with the conventional saloon rounded wheelarches, not the sportier flared variety.

To the delight of spectators, racing driver Russ Swift was also a regular site at GM Dealer Sports days in the mid-1980s, bravely demonstrating a fascinating display of

The Nova Sport brochure cover.

pirouetting Nova hatchbacks, and also driving Astramax vans on two wheels following many hours of practice ... with passengers queueing to have a ride.

Peter Hutchinson, an engineer and Vauxhall fan in the mid-1980s, converted several Nova saloons into attractive T-Bar roofed cabriolets with Vauxhall's blessing after parking his converted Carmine Red example outside a Vauxhall conference at a hotel, where, the story goes, he took nine orders that day. It is unclear how many of these survive. "Add a dash of excitement to your Nova two-door saloon ..." stated the sales flyer. Models were sold through local dealers in Hertfordshire. Further independent conversions were offered on the Nova hatch, too.

In 1988, the SR sported a new specific front grille and spoilers. Wheel covers were now anthracite (similar to those seen on recently deleted Monza GSE) and there was heat insulating green tinted glass. All models had a more convenient tailgate handle, and the whole vehicle was freshened up inside.

Diverting through heavy traffic in a red five-door hatch, the hit single *La Bamba* (performed by Ritchie Valens) played in TV adverts. This was used again as a soundtrack for the later Nova GTE. Play it on YouTube, you will be humming it for hours ...

For several months starting in June 1988, a 'Hot Metal' heavy marketing campaign introduced the £8185 Nova GTE. Pitched

The late 1980s Nova GTE always was on a three-door hatchback platform. (Courtesy Lindon Lait)

The non-injected 1.5-litre diesel Nova with its face-lifted five-door hatchback shell.

A muddy press advert for the Nova GSi rally car.

Entry level Nova Trip interior.

heavily against the Fiesta XR2 and MG Metro Turbo, the new GTE utilised the 1.6-litre injected engine. Over the SR, GTE upgrades included sunroof, sports seats, aerodynamic sill mouldings, body-coloured front grille and spoilers plus 175/65 HR14 low profile tyres. In 1988, *Autocar* magazine pitched the GTE against the XR2 and Daihatsu Charade GT Ti. "Who makes the best XR2? It's not Ford"

A Novavan was available with the face-lifted bodyshell. It was introduced after the Bedford name was dropped, so was always badged as a Vauxhall.

was the front cover teaser: the Nova beat the competition on all counts, with the best top speed (119mph), fuel economy, seats, fail-safe handling, equipment level and quietness.

For the forthcoming 1990 model year the 1.3-litre engine was uprated to 1.4-litre, an increase of 2hp. Interiors and exteriors continued largely unchanged, but sound deadening was improved. The 1.5-litre turbo diesel engine was offered from late 1989 in three-door form for the following year, this being a zippy little DERV to compete head-on with the Metro, Fiesta, 106 and Citroën AX small block diesels. The Nova 1.5 TD came with a rev counter and five-speed gearbox, so was well equipped, and a creditable 70mpg could be attained at a constant 56mph. Worthy of note here was the non-turbo 1.5D that arrived later for the 1992 model year, being £860 cheaper and achieving about 3mpg more in overall economy.

Details of the entire Nova range improvements were published in autumn 1990. The improved cars were easy to spot, with new smooth bumpers and revised grilles. White turn indicators and revised headlamps completed the new front look, whilst the interiors boasted new trims and colours, plus a new switch gear and soft touch facias. Those new headlamps could be electronically adjusted across the range. The Nova Trip became the new 1-litre entry level model, and the Flair (previously a limited edition) a mid-range model with bright trim and colour offerings "for the extrovert ...". At this time the GTE was effectively replaced with a new top sports model, the GSi, still with the 1.6-litre engine with an identical power output, and all the newest modifications and Rio cloth trim throughout. The top-mounted tailgate spoiler was simplified and still colour coordinated. The two-door saloons were discontinued at this time.

The Novavan was only ever badged as a Vauxhall (never as Bedford), as it arrived in late 1990 along with the Nova face-lift, although earlier style Opel Corsa van types were available from the start of production on the continent. Engine availability with the van was standard diesel 1.5-litre or the 1.2-litre petrol.

The SR had improvements early in 1992, gaining a 14 per cent boost in power and becoming the 1.4 SRi with a slick five-speed close ratio gearbox. Additional models included the Nova Luxe Plus and the SX. The Nova finally disappeared from the price lists in 1993, making way for the all-new Corsa.

Certainly the Nova was king of special editions. Although possibly not definitive, here is what research brings up. Year availability follows each type: Sport, Swing (1984), Casanova (1986), Antibes, Club (all white) (1987), Flair, Gem (1988), Diamond (1988-90), Invader, Pearl (four-door), Star, Sting (1989), Cricket (white only), Life (1991), Spin (1991-92), Novavan SRv & GSv (1992), Fun, Luxe Plus, Snap (1992), Expression, Swing II (1992-93).

Nova media advertising slogans

Fiorucci to Gucci in 4.8 minutes
Announcing our weekend body building course (1985 accessories)
Engineered for rugged dependability
The car is hairy. The price, shaved (Sport)
The spin. It's a snip (Spin)
Powa Nova (SRi)
Posha Nova (Luxe Plus)
Meana Nova (1.5 TD)
Turning heads and winning hearts (CasaNova limited edition)
Sun and fun in 45 seconds (cabriolet conversion)
More bits. Less bobs (Diamond & Swing)
We just couldn't leave well enough alone
One small car where the boot doesn't take a back seat (saloon)
Add some pepper to your performance (SR)
Macho for not mucho (SR)
Small, yet handles well over a ton (SR)
Ideal for getting to school on time
Anyone this loaded must have a Nova
Phew! And far between (Swing)
The more pounds you shed, the better you'll look accessories
The little better car
The nippy Nova. Now with improved dash (Flair)
Get a Nova on your cash-point card (Diamond)
Hot metal (GTE)
Star of the rally (GTE)

NOVA BODY TYPES: two-door saloon, four-door saloon, three-door hatch, five-door hatch, van: 1983-1993, some convertibles; **manufactured at**: Spain; **number produced**: 446,462
PERFORMANCE: **top speed**: 89mph (146kph)**; 0-60mph (100kph)**: 18 sec (1.2-litre); **average economy**: 35-50mpg
PRICE AT LAUNCH: £3635 (1-litre hatch)
MEASUREMENTS: length hatch/saloon: 11ft 10½in/12ft 9.7in (3.62/3.90m); **width**: 5ft½in (1.54m); **height**: 53½in (1.36m); **wheelbase**: 92.2in (2.34m); **weight**: 1708-1983lb (775-900kg); **wheels**: 13 &14in; **suspension**: independent MacPherson coil (front), progressive miniblock coil (rear); **turning circle**: 30.7ft (9.32m); **fuel capacity**: 9.2 gallons (42 litres); **boot capacity**: 7.9ft^3 (hatch)
TECHNICAL: **engine types**: 993, 1196, 1297, 1389, 1598cc, four-cyl, petrol, 1488cc four-cyl, diesel; **gearbox**: four-speed & five-speed manual, **front-wheel drive**
TRIM: cloth, velour
KEY OPTIONAL EXTRAS: towing equipment, metallic paint, fog lamps

Corsa Mk1

The name Corsa had been used previously by Opel for its version of the UK's Nova, and just as Opel took the UK Astra name, the Vauxhall took the Corsa name for its replacement of the Nova, launching the new model in February 1993. This was an entirely different vehicle. Gone was the boxy shape of the Nova, in favour of a more rounded line, and two bodyshells were employed: the three-door and five-door hatchback only. Engine line-up was 1.2, 1.2E, 1.4, 1.6 16v and the 1.5 diesel in both turbo and non-turbo form, as per previous Novas. Immediately obvious was the greater cabin room compared to its predecessor, with big increases in wheelbases and track.

The heavily marketed range was supported by its 'Supermodel' advertising campaign, the early 1.4 Si appeared regularly in adverts but was deleted in 2000. Later in 1993, five odd ball double-page magazine and billboard poster adverts ran using different famous supermodels abusing a Corsa; sledgehammer safety cage test, giant industrial claw, concrete mix through the sunroof, wrecker's swing-ball on hefty chain and a bucket of lurid green paint over a white car. Media marketing was certainly changing ...

Corsa model line up by 1995 was Merit (later Envoy in 1999), SRi (replaced by SXi in

Several adverts depicting supermodels trashing new Corsas were carefully produced by the Vauxhall agency. Here, Linda gleefully throws a bucket of green paint at a 1.2i Merit.

Following the supermodel launch (see text), the five-door advert makes reference to the event in London.

Corsa production line in Spain.

Vauxhall promoted the Corsa as the perfect driving school car. Here is a five-door being put to such use.

Corsa colourful interior treatment.

1998), LS, GLS, Sport, CDX, summer 1993 entry GSi 16v (gone by 1996). The Mk1 Corsa lasted until 2000, following a face-lift in 1997.

Corsa limited editions included: Swing (1994), Arizona (1995), Montana (1995), Spin (1995), Twist (1995), Breeze (1994-on), Premier, (1996), Club (1999), Vegas (1996) and Trip (1996-on). Although outside the scope of this book, a smart 1.4-litre Corsa cabriolet was marketed from 1998, and the normally-aspirated 1.7-litre diesel was added in 1998. The SXi hatch joined in 1999.

The Corsa SRi 16v.

Corsa vans

In late 1993 the Combo van (a high roof) took over where the Astramax Mk2 van left off, and by 1994 the Corsavan took over where the previous Novavan left off. Both vans were available in 1.7 D Merit (with vinyl seats), and 1.4 petrol LS and 1.7 D LS, with later GLS version, and the van's production times shadowed that of the cars. A five-speed gearbox was standard. Maximum payload was 700kg, and the vans were popular with Royal Mail.

Corsa Mk1 media advertising slogans

Naomi happily demonstrates the Corsa's side impact bars
Christy has concrete proof no rival beats the Corsa for interior space
Linda christens this Corsa the most environmentally sound car in its class
So safe, it will even protect you from high insurance rates
Tatjana can't wait to test the Corsa's all round safety cage
Kate finds a tiny flaw in the Corsa's anti-theft system
Bold, confident, fun. Shouldn't all cars be like that?
The biggest small car we've ever built
It's finally seen off the competition (five-door)
Twist without going bust (Twist)
Handles life beautifully (SRi)

CORSA Mk1 BODY TYPES: Corsa Mk1 body types available: three-door hatch, five-door hatch, three-door van (incl high roof Combo), three-door cabriolet: 1993-1998; **manufactured at**: Zaragoza, Spain and Eisenach, Germany.
PERFORMANCE: **top speed**: 90/119mph (147/195 kph) (1-litre/1.6-litre GSi); **0-60mph (100kph)**: 18/8.7 sec; **average economy**: 30-45mpg.
PRICE AT LAUNCH: £6495 (Merit).
MEASUREMENTS: **length**: 12ft 2¾in (3.73m); **width**: 5ft 3¼in (1.61m); **height**: 4ft 8in (1.42m); **wheelbase**: 8ft ¼in (2.44m); **weight**: 1888-2263lb (857-1029kg); **wheels**: 13 & 14in; **turning circle**: 32.2ft (9.8m); **fuel capacity**: 10.1 gallons (46 litres); **boot capacity**: 9.2ft^3.
TECHNICAL: **engine types**: 973, 1195, 1389, 1598cc four-cyl petrol, 1488, 1686cc four-cyl diesel; **gearbox**: four- & five-speed manual, four-speed auto; **suspension**: independent MacPherson coil (front), progressive miniblock coil (rear); **brakes**: front disc, rear drum.
TRIM: vinyl (van), cloth, velour, leather.
KEY OPTIONAL EXTRAS: grey leather seats, ABS, air-conditioning, automatic gearbox, passenger airbag, metallic paint, alarm.

Tigra

Hot on the heels of the announcement of the Corsa, Project 4202, a Corsa two-plus-two coupé, was leaked to the press that same summer. The bright red Opel-badged exhibit was described as a mini Calibra, and even wore correct Tigra motifs at this stage. To get any chance of production, the concept had to get favourable public reaction. A bright red example was shown to an enthusiastic audience at the September 1993 Frankfurt Motor Show in Germany along with a bottle green Traka, an open top Lotus co-developed roadster leisure concept vehicle, and the Scamp, another attractive variation. More showings followed at the Earl's Court London Motor Show and the Tokyo Show in Japan, once the home of one of its GM designers, Hideo Kodama. The Tigra's distinctive wrap-round glass canopy styling, twin air-bags, side intrusion beams, alarm, deadlocks and first aid cubby box were received well. It was surprisingly wide (at nearly six feet) compared to other small GM products, and Vauxhall's estimate of 124mph top speed turned out to be rather optimistic!

Twelve months later, the Tigra had been launched as a new model in Barcelona (indeed its forward production was to be in northern Spain) for both the UK and continental markets and was ready for sale by the end of that year, rivalling the nifty Nissan 100 NX. The Tigra body was longer, lower and wider than the Corsa, but shared the same wheelbase and track. There were body curves everywhere, concave and convex, and not one panel was shared with the Corsa. Both Ecotec family fuel-injected 1.4- and 1.6-litre engines were offered, the latter giving an extra 16hp and

The Tigra was first revealed to the public at show-time, 1993.

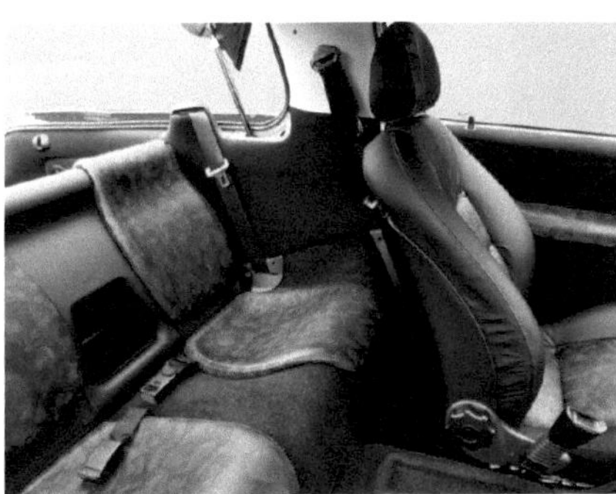

The prototype concept Tigra motor show cars in 1993 were attractively trimmed.

The Tigra was launched in 1994 and made great use of curved glass.

16v. US Sundym tinted solar glass was fitted to reduce interior temperatures – its first fitment in a European car. Interestingly, no engine sizes were advertised on the panels, although the larger-engined car could be identified by front fog lamps fitted as standard, a steel sliding pop-up sunroof and wider low profile tyres. The rear compartment was small – very small, but not as poor as MGB GT standards – and fitted with twin rear seatbelts; it was not recommended for passengers taller than 5ft 3in! Overall the Tigra entered new territory, giving high style at an affordable price (the entry price was around £11,000 in the UK), with novel sales brochures aiming at the younger population.

At the UK NEC Motor Show in October 1994, the new car proved a crowd-puller, described by *Autocar* as "as infectious to drive as it was to look at". It was not long before a

Marketing fun in Germany with the Opel Tigra.

The Tigra engine.

Curvy rear of a 1.4 Tigra.

1.6-litre 16v version joined the long-term test fleet.

At launch, UK comedian Harry Enfield was contracted to narrate daring TV adverts, and supporting press adverts followed. "Do you plump up the cushions on your sofa? Are you fond of milky drinks before bedtime? Do you take extra vitamins in cold weather? People who answer 'yes' won't like the new Tigra at all." Throughout the 1990s, contemporary brochures were splashed with large typeface words such as "Enjoy, Fun, Miaow, Psst, Whizz, Gee, Gotcha, Ouch", etc, and even Opel ran an *Italian Job* style advert in 1994 with a blue example driving the sewers of New York to avoid heavy traffic.

Ford responded with its similar-looking Puma in 1997, aimed at the same marketplace. By July 2001, the cheeky Mk1 Tigra had stopped production, with a new bigger Mk2 Tigra Twin Top offered three years later. There had been various limited edition models over its seven year production run including: MTV Summertime Limited Edition (1995), Twist (1995), Blue (1996), Premier (1996), Verde (1996), Marine (1997), Bermuda (1997) and Chequers (1998). It had also been sold as a Chevrolet Tigra in Brazil and Mexico but was not marketed in the USA.

The marketing department was proud of its rear end design ...

An Opel Tigra under test.

Rear passenger area, whilst attractive, could only be described as restricted – and for two occupants only!

Tigra media advertising titles
The power of design
Fun if you like that sort of thing
Sticks to corners (Billboard advert)
Do you iron creases into your jeans?
Do you always fold your pyjamas?

TIGRA BODY TYPES: three-door 2+2 coupé: 1994-2001; **manufactured at**: Zaragoza, Spain.
PERFORMANCE: **top speed**: 118/126mph (194/210kph 1.4-litre/1.6-litre); **0-60mph (100kph)**: 10.5/9.5 sec; **average economy**: 30-45mpg.
PRICE AT LAUNCH: £10,995 (1.4-litre).
MEASUREMENTS: **length**: 12ft 10½in (3.92m); **width**: 5ft 11¼in (1.81m); **height**: 4ft 4¾in (1.34m); **wheelbase**: 8ft¼in (2.44m); **weight**: 2368lb (1075kg); **wheels**: 14 & 15in; **turning circle**: 34ft 6in (10.5m); **fuel capacity**: 10.1 gallons (46 litres); **boot capacity**: 7.42ft^3.
TECHNICAL: **engine types**: 1389, 1598cc, four-cyl petrol; **gearbox**: five-speed manual; **suspension**: independent MacPherson coil (front), torsion beam, coils (rear); **brakes**: disc front, drum rear.
TRIM: deco cloth.
KEY OPTIONAL EXTRAS: metallic paint.

The limited edition MTV Tigra.

The limited edition Tigra Marine of 1997.

A very late model Tigra.

An Irmscher body Chequers limited edition Tigra.

The limited edition Chequers interior.

4x4 Frontera and Monterey

Frontera

The off-road leisure market was growing fast in the late 1980s, and Land Rover responded with its cheaper version of the Range Rover, the Discovery, in 1989. In 1991, General Motors released its trendy and slightly smaller Frontera off-roader, offered in both very trendsetting three-door short wheelbase sport form, and as a five-door longer wheelbase called the estate, with ongoing production at Luton. As it turned out, it was outsold by Land Rover's newer baby, the Freelander. However, in-house the Frontera's subsequent sales both sandwiched and outsold the bigger Monterey 4x4 model by a factor of 20.

A near identical Opel Frontera was also sold in Europe. It offered a step-down low transfer gearbox (sport and estate had different ratios), and, unlike the Land Rover, the high range was rear-wheel drive only. A Mk2 Frontera with fresh body panels was sold from 1998, and this continued until 2004.

The range was updated in 1995, receiving progressive rate rear coil suspension to replace the old cart-sprung semi-elliptic models and a new range of engines. In addition, the sport could be ordered with a diesel. In 1996-97, the VM 2499cc diesel (also seen in the economy specification Range Rovers) was fitted. During its production, the Frontera was offered as the following limited editions: Diamond 1993 & 1995/6 (LWB), Glacier 1994 (LWB), Nautilus 1994 (LWB), Apache 1995 (SWB), San Diego 1997 (LWB), Niagra 1997 (SWB) and the model run-out Transglobe 1998 (on both wheelbases). Unlike the Monterey, the Frontera received plenty of press advertising.

At time of writing (2022) there are only 1237 Fronteras taxed and 'on the road' in the UK, with another 4773 taxed as 'off the road,' out of a total of nearly 52,000 built. The first figures include the Mk2, making surviving Mk1 Fronteras quite scarce ...

Frontera media advertising slogans
Whole new engine. Whole new suspension. Whole new world (1995)
Escape in style in the new Vauxhall Frontera (1991)
See a totally new world in a totally new Frontera (1991 x 2)
Country Strife
Buy a Frontera. Get a free driving course on the side (1991)
Just popping up the road for some milk honey (San Diego)

The Frontera sport, always in short wheelbase form.

The Frontera sport rivalled the SWB Land Rover Freelander, but was aimed at a younger, more outgoing customer base.

A tow car for gliders anyone? Early Frontera sport.

The longer five-door Frontera 'estate' was also put to police patrol use.

The well-appointed interior of a 1996 five-door Frontera.

It's not the travel news you need. It's the shipping forecast (1995)
Burn some rubber this weekend (1995)

FRONTERA BODY TYPES: three-door sport (SWB), five-door estate (LWB): 1991- 1998 (Mk1); **manufactured at**: Luton; **number produced**: 51,925.
PERFORMANCE: SWB petrol/LWB diesel; **0-60mph (100kph)**: 14 sec/19.3 sec, **Top speed**: 98mph/91mph (155/145kph); **average economy**: 22-29mpg.
PRICE AT LAUNCH: £12,250 (SWB petrol), £16,830 (LWB diesel).
MEASUREMENTS: **length**: 13ft 9in (4.19m) (SWB), 15ft 5in (4.71m) (LWB); **width**: 5ft 10in (1.78m); **height**: 5ft 6½in (1.69m) (SWB), 5ft 7¼in (1.71m) (LWB); **wheelbase**: 7ft 7½in (2.33m) (SWB), 9ft½in (2.76m) (LWB); **weight**: 3440lb (1561kg) (SWB), 3931lb (1784kg) (LWB); **wheels**: 15/16in; **turning circle**: 32ft 4in (9.87m) (SWB), 37ft 5in (11.41m) (LWB); **fuel capacity**: 17.6 gallons (80 litres); **boot capacity**: 0.42/1.16m^3 (seats up/folded) (SWB).
TECHNICAL: **engine types**: 1998cc, four-cyl then X20 (year 1995) & 2410cc, four-cyl (petrols), 2260cc four-cyl 2499cc (VM), 2771cc, four-cyl (diesels); **gearbox**: five-speed manual, plus transfer gearbox with low ratio; **suspension**: independent double wishbone, torsion bar (front), rigid axle, semi-elliptic springs then (from 1995) progressive rate coils (rear); **brakes**: disc all round.
TRIM: cloth.
KEY OPTIONAL EXTRAS: various including tow bar.

Monterey

Research for this book reveals that this is the second least publicised and road tested Vauxhall, running second behind the Albany! Press rumours had circulated about this car in late 1991. Bigger than the existing, more popular Frontera, the late entry 1994 Monterey was brought in to kick at the heels of the five-year-old Land Rover Discovery, and was offered in petrol and diesel form in both three-door short wheelbase (RS) and (at 17in longer) five-door long-wheelbase (LTD seven-seater) formats.

Opel introduced its identical Monterey at the same time, using the same Californian coastal town name that had been borrowed by the US Mercury for models in the 1950s-1970s. No surprise that this was a rebadged version of the ubiquitous second generation Isuzu Trooper (which was also sold in the UK), with a splash of chrome, velour trim to replace the rough and ready Trooper's tweed, and with different paintwork options. The Isuzu's importer started legal action against Vauxhall over its right to compete in the UK market, which was then settled out of court. The Trooper's sales were then restricted in future years, to be replaced by the Ssangyong off-roader. Globally, the vehicle also sold as an Opel, Acura, Holden, Honda, HSV, Sanjui, Subaru, Chevrolet and SsangYong between 1991 and 2002.

On launch, the Monterey was £3000 cheaper than the top specification ES

The low-volume selling Monterey was basically a rebadged second series Isuzu Trooper. This is the more common long wheelbase version.

The luxury Monterey interior to rival the Range Rover and top-end Discovery.

Very rarely seen, a short wheelbase Monterey RS. Yes, it is a Vauxhall, not an Isuzu Trooper! Location is Portmeirion, North Wales.

Discovery, and a lot cheaper than the prestigious Range Rover Vogue. Magazine advertising concentrated on the height of the vehicle – "Put your family above everything else" – similar to some Land Rover campaigns of the time. It was only sold through the 269 specialist Vauxhall 4x4 dealers. Even before launch, a soft-top RS sports design was studied, based on the shorter wheelbase platform, but this did not come to fruition. The Monterey Diamond was the most fully equipped model.

Using howmanyleft.co.uk online reveals just 139 taxed examples remain on UK roads. UK registrations were around 1600 diesels and 860 petrol versions (90 per cent of the petrol types sold were automatic), meaning it actually outsold the old, poor-selling 1980s Viceroy, becoming the second lowest selling Vauxhall (with its own unique bodyshell). When discontinued, the similar Opel-badged version continued in the continent. Some police forces used cars such as Cumbria and Bedford, and Vauxhall also marketed an ambulance version.

Press coverage was low: *Complete Car* tested it against Mitsubishi, Range Rover and Jeep in its June 1994 issue, and there was a brief drive by *Autocar* magazine in 1994. An online search revealed this particular vehicle lasted 14 years until passing its last MoT at 175,000 miles, but with the advisory that "... the steering felt vague on the road ..."

A Sunday newspaper tests the new LWB Monterey off-road, Vauxhall even had an off-road driving club at this point.

following a long failure list on items such as corrosion and leaks.

The shorter wheelbase diesel Monterey was deleted from the range by 1997, soon followed by the petrol RS SWB, and the LWB was available until 1998.

Monterey media advertising slogans
Put your family above everything else (LTD)
The height of Luxury (LTD)
The new Monterey from Vauxhall says high (Diamond)

MONTEREY BODY TYPES: three-door SWB, five-door LWB: 1994-1998; **manufactured at**: Tokyo; **number produced**: approx 2460 (see text).
PERFORMANCE: **top speed**: 106mph (170kph) V6, 94mph (150kph) diesel; **0-60mph (100kph)**: 10.7 sec (V6), 16.6 sec (diesel); **average economy**: 17-23mpg.
PRICE AT LAUNCH: £21,675/£23,290 (both petrol/diesel three-/five-door models).
MEASUREMENTS: **length**: 14ft 0in (4.27m) (SWB), 15ft 6½in (4.74m) (LWB); **width**: 5ft 6in (1.67m); **height**: 72.3in (1.84m); **wheelbase**: 7ft 6½in (2.3m) (SWB), 9ft½in (2.76m) (LWB); **weight**: 3956lb (1795kg) (SWB), 4375lb (1985kg) (LWB); **wheels**: 16in; **turning circle**: 38ft/11.58m (LWB/SWB); **fuel capacity**: 18.7 gallons (85 litres); **boot capacity**: 53ft^3 (folded SWB).
TECHNICAL: **engine types**: 3059cc, four-cyl, (diesel), 3165cc V6, (petrol); **gearbox**: five-speed manual with transfer box, overdrive option, four-speed automatic; **suspension**: double wishbone, torsion bar, coils (front), live multi-link axle, coils (rear); **brakes**: disc all round.
TRIM: velour, leather (on Diamond).
KEY OPTIONAL EXTRAS: third row of seats on LWB, air-conditioning, two-tone paint, four-speed automatic transmission, air-conditioning.

Towards the millennium

Omega

With the demise of the Carlton/Senator ranges in 1994, the slightly larger Omega took their combined places, with a revised engine range and deletion of the previous straight six engine. The new car was no big secret; several times over the previous few years pictures had been leaked to the press. The old cam-in-head engines were replaced by 54 degree 'V' formation 2.5-litre and 3-litre for the petrol cars (plus 8v and 16v 2-litre for entry level models), and a 2.5-litre turbo BMW diesel was also marketed. They offered a slight improvement in power and torque and measurable improvements in emissions, economy and weight, and the 2.5-litre had the advantage of fitting in other cars such as the Cavalier and Calibra, too. The latter, with its superb Cd figure, was followed closely by the new Omega at a creditable 0.29 Cd drag factor.

Automatic could be specified across the range (although standard on the CDX and Elite models), and the 'Economy,' 'Sports' and 'Driving' modes were continued from previous V-cars. New speed-sensitive steering was offered, and a sensor caused an audible alarm to go off if there was fog less than 200 yards ahead. Given its large size, the Omega was converted by specialist firms for limousine and hearse use, and many survive given their careful low mileages. In addition, Vauxhall was again promoting the Omega for police use, and as a motorway patrol car it proved very worthy. The marketeers homed in on its unique separate subframe-mounted multi-link suspension system "... that can cope with any road conditions." A space-saving spare wheel was now offered. The press was comparing the new Omega with the Rover Sterling, Mercedes-Benz C-Class, BMW 5-series, Ford Scorpio and top Volvo products, often very favourably.

Body styles were a four-door saloon and a spacious five-door estate version, and came

The Omega CD estate.

The Omega MV6 saloon.

The Omega CDX saloon.

in (ascending order) Edition S, Select, GLS, CD, CDX, Elite and later MV6 trim packages. The first edition, Omega B1, was updated to the B2 in 1999 with minor revisions to the front and rear styling. The Omega evolved with further new engines until its demise in 2004, after 65,840 (earlier versions) had been produced.

Omega media advertising slogans

It has a built-in device that reduces the engine noise. It's called the engine

Power and manoeuvrability. Important assets for any executive

... has multi-link suspension that can cope with any road conditions

Perfect for taking far flung corners (estate)

OMEGA BODY TYPES: four-door saloon, five-door estate: 1994-2004; **manufactured at**: Russelsheim, Germany; **number produced**: 65,840.

PERFORMANCE: **top speed**: 149mph (230kph) (3-litre); **0-60mph (100kph)**: 8.3 sec; **average economy**: 24-35mpg (model dependant).

PRICE AT LAUNCH: £16,486 to £27,441.

MEASUREMENTS: **length**: 15ft 8½in/4.79m (saloon), 15ft 9¾in/4.82m (estate); **width**: 5ft 10¼in (1.78m); **height**: 4ft 9¼in/1.45m (saloon), 5ft 0¾in/1.54m (estate); **wheelbase**: 8ft 11½in (2.73m); **weight**: 3090-2440lb (1400-1590kg); **wheels**: 15in; **turning circle**: 33ft 6in (10.2m); **fuel capacity**: 16.5 gallons (75 litres); **boot capacity**: 0.5m^3.

TECHNICAL: **engine types**: 1998cc, four-cyl, 8 & 16v, 2498, 2962cc, 24v V6 (petrol), 2498cc (diesel); **gearbox**: five-speed manual, four-speed automatic; **suspension**: independent coil with MacPherson strut (front), independent multi-link (rear); **brakes**: disc all round.

TRIM: velour, leather.

KEY OPTIONAL EXTRAS: rear levelling suspension, cruise control, metallic paint (on certain non equipped models), leather seats, roof rack, estate load cage, tow hitch.

Vauxhall beyond 1995 ...

Beyond the scope of this book, there were further Astras and Tigras, the Insignia replaced the Omega, the Vectra replaced

The Vectra took over where the Cavalier Mk3 left off.

The much-loved Lotus-built VX 220 Turbo.

the Cavalier, then the Signum replaced the Vectra, and Vauxhall entered the MPV sector with the US-built eight-seater Sintra, the Zafira and little Meriva. Not forgetting the mighty Monaro ...

The VX220 was a remarkable two-seater sports car produced between 2001 and 2005 by Lotus cars in Hethel, Norfolk, with a 0-60mph of an advertised 5.6 seconds. "Strapped in and stretched out, your body will thrill to every mile. We reckon it looks even better than the Lotus," stated *What Car?* magazine – mission accomplished. Despite popular belief, less than 10 per cent of the VX220 components were interchangeable with the Elise.

Soon after this we saw the super 'hot' 2004-2018 VXR range with a dedicated advertising programme; these were the boy racers' transport of the 2000s: Corsa VXR, Corsa VXR Arctic Edition, Corsa VXR Nürburgring, Meriva VXR, Astra VXR, Astra VXR Nürburgring, Monaro VXR, Insignia VXR, Vectra VXR, Zafira VXR, VXR8, VXR8 Bathurst and VXR220 ... perhaps worthy of another volume!

Interior of the two-seater VX 220.

Vauxhall joined the MPV arena with the Zafira in 1999 after the poor-selling Sintra was dropped after just three years.

Appendix 1

Racing and rallying Vauxhalls

Early rallying

In the postwar years, some brave privateers entered their Vauxhall cars in key motorsport events across the production era covered by this book, although compared to all the British Jaguar, Ford, Hillman, Sunbeam, Mini, Allard, Austin-Healey, MG, Rover, Austin and Morris cars, Vauxhall numbers look a little low.

In January 1938, a Norwegian from Stavanger competed in the Monte Carlo Rally in a Vauxhall Ten without the loss of a single mark on this road event, and placed second overall. In the early 1950s, when rallying resumed following the war, L-Type Velox and Wyverns were entered, and E-Type Crestas and Veloxes were seen in various Monte Carlo rallies (sometimes prepared by Shaw & Kilburn Ltd of London). A Velox was entered in the Coronation Rally in Kenya in the 1950s, as its engine could easily be tuned to 100hp by the specialists. In 1959, an Irish privateer entered a Victor Super in the Monte Carlo Rally, followed by a PA Cresta in the 1960 event, which took second in class. An army team entered a PA Velox in the 1961 RAC Rally.

The new VX4/90 was a regular sight on several events: the Monte Carlo Rally and RAC Rally in 1963 and 1964, and the 1963 Tulip Rally. In 1965 the 3.3-litre Cresta made its world debut on the Circuit of Ireland Rally, where Ken Shields took it to best in class. Later in the decade a Viva HB and a Ventora FD took part in the lengthy London to Sydney Marathon, whilst back home many Bill Blydenstein-tuned Vivas were used as track cars, and had become regular sightings by the 1970s when DTV – Dealer Team Vauxhall – was formed. Bill Blydenstein had cut his racing teeth years before with the unlikely Borward Isabella, but became a force to be reckoned with when it came to Vauxhall-tuning from the mid-1960s.

The 1970s

With much grace, Gerry Marshall drove the Old Nail Firenza, notching up 65 outright wins between 1971 and 1975, then for six months

Left to right: Des Donelly, Jim Thompson, Bill Dryden and Gerry Marshall with their racing Viva GTs at Ellesemere Port in 1971.

Tuner Bill Blydenstein at his Shepreth works poses on the old railway station platform with Gerry Marshall.

he also drove Big Bertha – the stunning 160mph/255kph Repco-Holden V8 Ventora, which suffered a high-speed accident at the Silverstone circuit in 1974 when a brake pad fell out. Baby Bertha, based on a Firenza shell that utilised the wrecked Big Bertha's mechanicals, was wheeled out only three times in 1975, but won on each occasion, and went on to dominate saloon car racing for a further three years. James Hunt and David Benson competed in the 1974 Avon Tour of Britain in their Magnum coupé, and another Magnum driven by Peter Brock in the 1977 Spa 24 Hour Race came second overall: the best continental racing result for Vauxhall since 1913.

The rest, as they say, is history, with the robust Chevette 2300HS becoming a regular sight at top European rallies (usually in distinctive silver metallic – remember

The James Hunt and David Benson Daily Express newspaper racing Magnum coupé entered in the 1974 Avon Tour of Britain. It retired due to an overheating engine, although Will Sparrow and Andrew Cowan secured 7th and 8th respectively in their Magnums.

The Old Nail racing Firenza on the track.

HSS975N?), and various cars with successful results driven by Pentti Airikkala, Chris Sclater, Tony Pond, Gerry Marshall and Jimmy McRae. In 1979, the Chevette HS won the gruelling British Open Rally Championship, followed by the British National Rally Championship, Irish Tarmac Championship and Scottish Championship in 1980.

Big Bertha, the Repco-Holden V8 based on the Ventora, was to crash spectacularly at Silverstone, but its mechanicals soon lived on in Baby Bertha.

Baby Bertha driven by Gerry Marshall.

A press advert after the Chevette HS began winning European rallies.

The 1980s & 1990s

The HSR continued the Chevette's success on the rally scene. Of special note, Jimmy McRae gained four wins in Irish events in 1980, and Tony Pond gained five wins in the 1981 season. Russell Brookes won the Circuit of Ireland in 1983.

Throughout the 1980s and early 1990s, the following drivers also competed successfully with Vauxhall Astras and Novas in different racing categories: Dave Metcalfe, Harry Hockly, Andrew Wood, Louise Aitken-Walker and Brian Wiggins. In 1989, the big Thundersaloon Carlton V8 pleased the large

A Chevette HSR competes on the Circuit of Ireland Rally.

Late 1980s Astra GTE.

Carlton Thundersaloon V8 track car.

A track-racing Cavalier GSi.

crowds at enclosed track events such as Snetterton.

Through to the 1990s, the Astra Mk3 fared well on the Network Q Rally and Mobil 1/ Top Gear British Rally Championship (won by David Llewellin) and the Cavalier Mk3 of John Cleland was a tarmac-track crowd puller in the mid-1990s BTCC, replaced by the Vectra in 1995 after the Cavalier's six seasons of racing.

Slightly beyond the scope of this book were other UK and overseas GM races, such as the Holden racing programme in Australia, the rally success of the Opel Manta and Ascona 400 cars, and the track prowess of the Opel Monza.

Mk3 Astra on the Perth Scottish Rally in 1992 with David Llewellyn.

Appendix 2

Vauxhall on the screen: TV and movie appearances

Vauxhall racing and rallying footage can be found online or on DVD, but what about films, TV programmes and old TV adverts? It's true that Vauxhalls don't make as many UK TV appearances as Fords or other key marques – generally the British Leyland press office propped up Pinewood Studios (*The New Avengers*, early episodes of *The Professionals*) and Ford many of the Euston productions (later *The Professionals, Minder, The Sweeney* etc) in the 1970s and 1980s. However, here is a very basic list of Vauxhall screen appearances, either alongside a main character or extensively throughout an episode or movie. Occasionally used vehicles, although good to see, are not included in this list, which is restricted to UK productions.

Apart from old TV and cinema adverts, amongst the best to seek out on YouTube, secondhand DVDs or online are:

Maggie Smith's character Miss Mary Shepherd living out of a 1957 Bedford CA – this van still survives after being auctioned in 2016 (Lady in a van); Rodney Bewes' character pulling a caravan in an early production red Chevette (HTM 10N) in *The Likely Lads* movie, also Rodney Bewes' character in the TV version in his Viva 1600 HB (ALF 132H); the *Doc Martin* character Bert Large squeezing into a red Bedford Rascal (at least two vans, the E170 ORL plumber's van believed to have been a rebadged Suzuki Super Carry) and E402 JJM (the restaurant vehicle, and still on the road having been auctioned off); many Astras and Cavaliers burning rubber in *The Bill,* and Vera Duckworth winning a red Vauxhall Nova in a 1980s episode of *Coronation Street.*

A personal author highlight has to be the private detective Jeff Randall's FD Victor RXD996F in *Randall & Hopkirk (Deceased),* the production team used a Ventora FD and the actor Kenneth Cope even quoted the registration number, but failed to note it was one digit out from his colleague's Victor! Both cars were fresh from the Vauxhall press pool in Luton. They call it product placement these days!

In alphabetical order of model:

10 – *Grantchester*

12 – *Mandy*

14 – *Just My Luck, The Dam Busters, Exodus, Aadmi, A Town Like Alice*

Astra Mk1 – *Minder, Some Mother's Son, The Bill, The Lady, Brookside* (GTE)

Astra Mk2 – *The Chief, London's Burning, The Bill, Floodtide*

Astra Mk3 – *The Bill, Dalziel and Pascoe, Wycliffe, A Touch of Frost, The Thin Blue Line,* plus Astramax (*Minder*)

Bedford CA – *The Lady in the Van, A Weekend with Lulu*

Bedford CF – *The Likely Lads* (1976 movie), *Stay Lucky, The London Connection, Spike Island*

Bedford Midi/Suzuki Super Carry – *Doc Martin, Ain't Misbehavin*

Bedford Rascal – *Spiceworld, Brassic*

Brava – *Lovejoy*

Calibra – *Finney, The Missing Postman, Spender, Boon, Like It Is*

Carlton – *Minder, Floodtide, White Gold, Mr Palfry of Westminster* (Mk1) plus *Prime Suspect, Bergerac, Cracker, A Year in Provence, The Hawk* (Mk2) & *Sharman* (Lotus)

Cavalier – *The Sweeney* (TV and movie), *Minder, The Professionals, 50 Dead Men Walking* (coupé) (Mk1), *The Bill, Minder, Boon, Brassed Off* (1985), *Bulman, Bergerac* (Mk2), *Lovejoy, Byker Grove, Cracker, A Mind to Kill, The Hawk* (Mk3)

Chevette – *The Likely Lads* (1976 movie), *Our Friends in the North, Doctor Who, At Home with the Braithwaites, Emmerdale Farm, Minder* (Chevanne)

Corsa – *Coronation Street, London's Burning, Another Year, One Foot in the Grave*

Cresta – *The Specials, Ghost Town* (music video), *Buddy's Song, On the Run* (PA), *The Saint, The Persuaders* (PB), *The Champions, The Saint* (PC)

Frontera – *London's Burning, Brookside, The Knock*

Magnum – *Red Riding: The Year of Our Lord 1974*

Monterey – *A Mind to Kill, Prime Suspect*

Nova – *Watching, Coronation Street, Bergerac, London's Burning, Drunken Money*

Randall & Hopkirk (Deceased) was a late 1960s science fiction drama that featured several Vauxhalls, particularly the FD Victor driven by the main character. What ever happened to RXD 996F? Pictured here is an identical FD.

The author was delighted to make the acquaintance of a Bedford Rascal van used in the TV drama Doc Martin, pictured here in Port Isaac, Cornwall, in 2017.

Royale saloon – *Minder* (plus a coupé in the later episode's opening titles)
Senator A – *Sylvia, The Beiderbecke Tapes*
Senator B – *The Bill, The Chief, G.B.H., The Bill, A Taste for Death*
Velox – *Alfie* (1966), *Miss Marple* (E), *The Rivals* (1963 movie), *The Saint, The Sweeney* (PB), *Taggart* (PC)
Ventora – *Department S,* T*he Professionals* (FD), *Drive Carefully Darling, Minder, Special Branch, The XYY Man, The Adventurer* (FE)
Victor F – *A Taste of Honey* (1961), *Spy, The Man From Uncle*
Victor FB – *Five to One, The Share Out, The Saint*
Victor FC – *A Moment's Reflection, The Scales of Justice, Craze, Stop, Strange Report*
Victor FD – *Randall & Hopkirk (Deceased), The Professionals, Department S, Heera Panna, Paul Temple, Dixon of Dock Green* (3300 police)
Victor FE – *The Dogs of War* (with false plates AXE586R), *The XYY Man, Special Branch*
Viscount – *The Saint, The Champions*
Viva HA – *Otley* (1968 movie) plus *Minder, A Fish Called Wanda, Beiderbecke Affair/Tapes/ Connection* (HA van), *The Chief, Strangers*
Viva HB – *The Sweeney, Whatever Happened to the Likely Lads, Bless this House, H-H-H-H, Shoestring*
Viva HC – *Jason King, Byker Grove, The Gentle Touch, Fox, Spearhead, Juliet Bravo*
VX4/90 – *The Saint* (FB), *The Champions, Pennyworth* (FC), *The Saint* (FD)
Wyvern (L series) – *Heartbeat, The Bletchley Circle*
Wyvern (E series) – *Invisible Man, Profile*

By the mid-1970s, car manufacturers had discovered the power of commercial TV advertising, and visibility increased moving forward from the stuffy 1960s campaigns. In 1974, whilst Martin Shaw had been seen advertising the new Mk2 Ford Capri and later washing powder, racing car driver James Hunt was employed by Vauxhall to push the four-year-old Viva, recommending a test drive "Tell them James Hunt sent you!" He went on to advertise the Chevette after winning the 1976 F1 World Championship title. The previously mentioned actor Rodney Bewes appeared in a 15-minute Vauxhall training film for the Chevette.

Other celebrities used were Shaw Taylor, Patrick McNee, dressed as his character John Steed from *The New Avengers* (all 1977 models), Harry Enfield's voice (Tigra), Penelope Keith, *The Bill*'s Larry Dann (Chevette Special), Tommy Godfrey (Viva HA), Jennifer Ehle, Tony Britton, Alastair McGowan, Liz Smith, Nigel Hawthorn and numerous others. Martin Shaw swopped sides and advertised the new Mk2 Cavalier LX in 1987 and the GM credit card in 1994 (standing aside a Calibra). From the late 1980s, Eric Clapton's song *Layla* was used extensively at the end of each commercial for a few brief bars. Most of these adverts have found their way on to YouTube, including later ones (outside the date range of this book) featuring comic Griff Rhys Jones. They are certainly worth a look, but do allow for many home recordings transferred from scratchy VHS format.

Racing driver James Hunt and promotion for the Chevette

Appendix 3

Small Bedford commercials

This appendix serves as a brief overview of the small Bedford commercial vehicles offered from 1945-1995, which did not form part of the main car range. Details of commercial applications of the H-Types, J-Types, Astravans, Combos, Bedford HAs, Chevannes, Corsavans and Novavans can be found in the specific car chapters. Note that the Bedford name was dropped on 1st June 1990, thus all commercial vehicles in this volume were badged as Vauxhall from that point.

Bedford CA

Fond memories of newspaper delivery vans, milk floats, minibuses, heavily laden grocers' shop vehicles and tuneful ice cream vendors come to immediate mind when thinking of the evergreen CA, now certainly regarded as a classic icon of the 1950s and 1960s. There were essentially three derivatives; 1952 to 1958 (10 & 12cwt), 1958 to 1964 and 1964 to 1969, when the CA project gave way to the bigger, more modern CFs. Most factory models had sliding doors, excluding those with a separate cab, such as the drop-side truck with its very pronounced front door hinges and rear access handles. It was convenient in the summer to drive with the sliding doors right back, and, if not secured, they would fly forward and shut upon heavy braking just in time to almost sever the alighting passengers arm!

There were quite a few small changes to the CA through its production run. Three types of windscreen were seen through the production life: early flat split screen on the Mk1, the second two types using curved glass, which became cheaper to produce as time went on, and even bigger, taller screens on the later models. For the 1963 model year, vans were offered in two lengths. A new longer version added 12in to the wheelbase and overall length, and thus the 15/17cwt versions were born. Various engines and gearboxes were borrowed from the contemporary Vauxhall saloon cars of the time, and two diesels were offered from the early 1960s onwards.

Martin Walter Converters in Folkestone offered its Utilicon people carrier from the early 1950s, and became instrumental in the sub-£700 camper van Dormobile Romany/Debonair conversions from 1957 onwards, starting a conversion trend that would last for decades. An interesting extra cost option from Martin Walter was fibre-glass rear fins to match the style of the Cresta/Velox PA range.

The Utilecon Martin Walter Bedford CA people carrier of the mid-1950s; this one a split-screen.

The early 1960s Bedford CA Utilabrake by Martin Walter. Note the later one-piece windscreen. Those rear fins were fake fibre-glass units, and optional.

CA BODY TYPES: enclosed van, camper-van, minibus, gown van, drop-side/all steel and canopy pick-ups, plus several specialist types. Production run: 1952-1969; **manufactured at**: Luton; **number produced**: over 370,000.
PERFORMANCE: **top speed**: 59mph (99kph) (Mk1 1507cc), 65mph (105kph) later versions; **0-50mph (84kph)**: 40 sec; **average economy**: 25-30mpg.
PRICE: £513 (panel van in 1957).
MEASUREMENTS: **length**: 12ft 10in/2.28m (SWB), 13ft 10in/2.59m (LWB); **width**: 70in/(1.78m); **height**: 74¾in/1.9m; **wheelbase**: 7ft 6in/8ft 4in (2.29/2.54m); **weight**: 2245lb

Photographed at a Volvo classic car meeting in Bridgnorth, 2022, is a 1963 Dormobile conversion on the Bedford CA, 1600cc petrol version.

Bedford CA Dormobile driver's compartment. Note at the top-left the sliding door, fitted to all CAs except chassis cab variants.

Side body chrome badging seen on two different Bedford CA Dormobile conversions.

A rather tidy early 1970s Bedford CF ice cream van in Chappel, Essex, summer 2022. Just visible behind is a Rascal ice cream van.

(1018kg); **wheels**: 13, 15 & 16in; **turning circle**: 34ft/10.36m (SWB), 37ft/11.28m (LWB); **fuel capacity**: 7½ gallons (34 litres); **internal capacity**: 135ft^3 (SWB).
TECHNICAL: **engine types**: 1508/1594cc four-cyl (petrol) & 1622/1760cc four-cyl (Perkins diesel); **gearbox**: three- & four-speed manual; **suspension**: double wishbone, coil (front), semi-elliptic (rear); **brakes**: drum.
TRIM: vinyl.
KEY OPTIONAL EXTRAS: automatic gearbox, numerous others.

Bedford CF

The CF continued the CA's trend of using Vauxhall saloon car petrol engines and gearboxes for light commercial use, and after a four-year design period was launched in October 1969 to an enthusiastic public at the UK Motor Show, becoming available for sale in 1970. This was the only Bedford van offered with a TK truck twin rear wheel axle to take the extra weight, with uprated suspension on such models. Again like the CA, the engine borrowed cab space, and for ease of servicing the rear was accessed by a removable cover. Petrols and diesel engines were offered, although the diesels were very slow! The cab was very airy and modern compared to its predecessor, and overall the CF was considerably wider and longer than the CA.

Major bodywork conversions to the Bedford CF were contracted out, such as this example.

The CF's main rivals were the better-selling Ford Transit and less popular Commer PB. It now had the new facility of front-hinged

The CF made a splendid base for camper-van conversions such as this Dormobile in a variety of guises, nearly always offered in petrol form.

cab doors, although some sliding door vans were still built for customers with tight access requirements, and they were also ideal in busy city deliveries. It came in three wheelbases, low roof, high roof, cab and chassis only option, and pick-up. A rugged 4x4 version (on 2.3-litre petrol versions from 1982) was offered by FF Developments, and many were converted into camper vans by several companies, plus there were many police and ambulance applications. In 1983, following several years in design an expensive 12v electric version was announced. It weighed nearly 2½ tons unladen, had a 50-60-mile range capability from its 40Kw motor, and heating was via a cab-mounted diesel generator ... The project was not successful, and was soon moved to the USA.

Adding to the general tradesman and grocer/butcher/baker, many corporations were key fleet buyers: the gas, water and electricity boards, Royal Mail, and Reddifusion TV to name a few.

The larger Victor FE slant-four petrol engines came in from 1972, replacing the earlier FD units. Front grilles went black for 1977, and the dashboard, dials and door cards were refreshed for the 1980 model year, including the use of plaid cloth trim on the seats, similar to the cars. However, the biggest visual change to the evolving CF was the complete change to the front and bumpers in October 1980. The new front end could be completely removed to further aid access to the engine.

The CF2 followed in May 1984 with further detail changes and the slant-four petrol engines were discontinued. New black door handles were used, bumpers altered once again, black grilles went grey and internal appointments were updated. Mk2 Astra wheel trims were fitted to some single wheel models. The CF was phased out year-end 1986, as sales were hardly booming – just 7881 were sold in 1985, partly caused by the new shape Ford Transit launched in the mid-1980s, and the availability of the new Midi and Rascal vans.

CF BODY TYPES: chassis cab, enclosed van, camper-van, minibus, gown van, drop-side, pick-up, etc: 1970-1986; **manufactured at**: Luton & CKD overseas; **number produced**: 501,764.

PERFORMANCE: for 35cwt 2279cc van, **Top speed**: 76mph (125kph); **0-50mph (80kph)**: 25 sec (diesels were considerably slower); **average economy**: 18-25mpg.

PRICE AT LAUNCH: £629 (14cwt van).

MEASUREMENTS: **length**: 17ft 1½in/4.3m (SWB van), 18ft 3in/5.57m (Glendale 6-birth caravan); **width**: 6ft 7½in/2.02m (van); **height**: 6ft 4¼in/1.93m (van); **wheelbase**: 8ft 10in/10ft 6in/11ft 8in (2.69/3.20/3.56m); **weight**: 890-1165kg; **wheels**: 13/14in; **turning circle**: 34ft 7in/10.54m (SWB van), 39ft 8in/12.1m (LWB); **fuel capacity**: 13 gallons (59 litres); **internal capacity**: 208/270ft^3.

TECHNICAL: **engine types**: 1599/1975cc then from March 1972 1759/2279cc four-cyl, then CF2 1979cc, four-cyl, 3.3-litre Holden engine with auto gearbox for ambulances (all petrol) & 1760/2524cc four-cyl (to 1975) then 2.1-litre Opel four-cyl from 1975-84, 2260cc (CF2), four-cyl (all diesels); **gearbox**: rarely seen three-speed manual to 1973, four-speed, four-speed ZF, five-speed ZF (manuals), three-speed GM Strasbourg automatic; **suspension**: coil (front), semi-elliptic (rear); **brakes**: front disc, drum rear.

TRIM: plastic, perforated Ambla or plaid cloth.

KEY OPTIONAL EXTRAS: many including automatic.

The Brava pick-up was badged as Bedford for two years, then became Vauxhall, replacing the ageing KB range in 1988. This pick-up is being put to good use in the early 1990s by linesmen from Southern Electric.

The KB was a rebadged Isuzu based on a worldwide platform. This is a face-lifted Bedford KB41 4x4 pick-up.

Later on, the Brava was available in crew-cab form, and known as the Doublecab.

KB & Brava pick-ups

The rugged Bedford KB started life as an early 1970s Isuzu Florian four-door saloon. The KB25 was a joint venture with Isuzu, which produced two different wheelbase versions, whereas UK cars started only with the long-wheelbase which was launched in 1980, a rival to the Ford P100 Cortina, Toyota and Mazda B1800 pick-ups that were getting increasingly popular. It was also sold in the USA as a Chevrolet. KB25 quickly became KB26 with a revised grille, headlamps, more modern dashboard and interior, and from 1982, a new KB41 model joined the range, with shorter wheelbase and selectable 4x4 transmission, and again either a diesel or petrol engine.

In October 1988, Bedford announced the introduction of the more modern Brava pick-up (a name also used by Fiat for a small passenger car), based on the next GM pick-up platform and also built in Japan. This rivalled the Ford P100 Sierra pick-up that had taken over from the Cortina P100 the previous year. Petrol-engined versions were dropped quite early on. A selectable 4x4 model was also made available, and this time both models shared the 3.02m wheelbase. Once again, badging went to Vauxhall from 1990, and was available as the Opel Campo in Germany. The Doublecab, a five-seater crew-cab version, was around from the 1994 season, as were the stylish Outback and Loader versions built for the leisure market sector.

KB/BRAVA BODY TYPES: pick-up: 1980-1988 (KB), 1988-2002 (crew-cab from 1994 on Brava); **manufactured at**: Fujisawa Kanagawa; **number produced**: KB a slow seller, Brava better.
PERFORMANCE: **top speed**: 71mph (114kph) diesel, 90mph (145kph) petrol (KB).
PRICE AT LAUNCH: £6010 (petrol) & £8750 (diesel 4x4) Brava.
MEASUREMENTS: **length**: 14ft 6in/15ft 11.3in (4.42/4.85m) (KB), 16ft 2in (4.92m) (Brava); **width**: 5ft 3in (1.60m) (KB), 5ft 6½in (1.69m) (Brava); **height**: 5ft 2¼in (1.58m) (KB), 5ft 3in-5ft 6½in (1.61-1.69m) (Brava); **wheelbase**: 9ft 11in (3.02m) (Brava); **weight**: 1305/1685kg (Brava 4x2 petrol/4x4 diesel Doublecab); **wheels**: 14in (4x2), 16in (4x4); **turning circle**: 11.8m (Brava 4x2), 12.2m (Brava 4x4); **fuel capacity**: 15.8 gallons (KB), 16.5 gallons/75 litres (Brava), 13.9 gallons/63 litres (Brava Doublecab).
TECHNICAL: **engine types**: 1584cc four-cyl petrol, 1951cc four-cyl diesel (KB25), 2254cc-litre, four-cyl petrol, 2238cc-litre/2499cc, four-cyl diesel (Brava); **gearbox**: four-speed then five-speed (KB), five-speed (Brava), 4x4s have two-speed transfer gears; **suspension**: independent with torsion bar springs (front), semi-elliptic (rear); **brakes**: front disc, rear drum.
TRIM: vinyl (KB), vinyl then grey velour (Brava).
KEY OPTIONAL EXTRAS: Brava: tiltable steering column, metallic paint.

Midi (& Albany)

Assembled from December 1984 at Luton and sold from March 1985 as part of a larger Isuzu WFR Fargo worldwide programme, the Bedford/Vauxhall Midi was available in two wheelbases with flip-up rear tailgate and passenger side sliding central door, on either an enclosed panel or fully glazed platform. There were people carriers and high roof versions in a 16-strong model range. From autumn 1988, a 4x4 option could be specified on the shorter vehicle (a 4x4 van display including Brava was shown at the October Motor Show), and diesels and petrol versions were available, with engines and gearboxes supplied directly from Isuzu. Each had a gross loaded vehicle weight of up to 3.3 tons, and, just like the 1950s Cresta days, a column gear change was used. Three abreast could be carried up-front if the triple seat option was specified. Dormobile and Hawson Garner were brought in to convert the Midi window van into a personnel carrier; a very cosy 15 people could be carried (five-row seating), whereas the factory SWB Midi could carry up to nine people in its 'estate' form.

With all Midis now badged as Vauxhall, the 1990 Motor Show was the launch platform for the upmarket Albany – effectively a well-trimmed SWB Midi with glazing, Vauxhall intended it to be a rival for the Renault Espace. Despite its upmarket Astra GTE velour rainbow trim, wood veneer dashboard, tinted glass, twin removable sunroofs, reclining front seats, swivelling/reclining central row seats and power steering, these very non van-like features were not enough to propel this now almost unheard-of vehicle into a high selling

The Midi could also be purchased as a people carrier with a variety of seating layouts.

Scarcely remembered, the Vauxhall Albany was an upmarket people carrier based on the Midi van with some fine interior appointments.

category. Around 300 petrol-only examples were registered in the UK, of which about two survive, possibly one of each of the two colours (Westminster Blue and Bordeaux Red) that were offered! Opening price at launch was £15,200, which matched the top line Cavaliers at the time. It vanished off the price lists by year end 1991.

The Midi continued with various cosmetic changes until the last 1995 model year, when a 2380cc turbo diesel replaced the other engines.

MIDI BODY TYPES: panel van, glazed van & high roof: December 1984-1996; **manufactured at**: Luton by Bedford then IBC; **number produced**: 115,096 (all UK brands).
PERFORMANCE: **top speed petrol/ diesel**: 81/73mph (132/120kph); **0-60mph (100kph)**: 22 sec (LWB 1.8-litre petrol high roof); **average economy**: 30mpg.
PRICE AT LAUNCH: £5535 + VAT (SWB petrol van).
MEASUREMENTS: **length**: 14ft 8½in & 15ft 9½in (4.48 & 4.82m) (SWB/LWB); **width**: 1.69m (both); **height**: 6ft 4½in & 7ft 2¼in (1.95 & 2.19m) (SWB/LWB); **wheelbases**: 7ft 8½in & 8ft 10in (2.35 & 2.69m) (SWB/LWB); **weight**: 2953/3108lb (1340/1410kg) (SWB petrol/diesel), 3054/3209lb (1386/1456kg) (LWB petrol/diesel); **wheels**: 14in; **turning circle**: 9.6/10.8m (SWB/LWB); **fuel capacity**: 13.2 gallons (60 litres).
TECHNICAL: **engine types**: 1817cc & 1994cc, four-cyl, (petrol), 1995cc (incl turbo) & 2189cc four-cyl (diesel); **gearbox**: five-speed manual; **suspension**: independent wishbones with coil (front), semi-elliptic (rear); **brakes**: front disc, rear drum.
TRIM: vinyl (no cost option), cloth (& velour in Albany).
KEY OPTIONAL EXTRAS: third front seat, nudge bar, sunroof, mud flaps, tow bar, power steering, load restraint eyes.

Rascal

Powered by the trusty Suzuki 970cc engine, and based on the 1979 Suzuki Super Carry, the tiny Rascal was launched in spring 1986 and enjoyed an eight-year production run at Luton, with owners reporting they drove anywhere – even between car park bollards! Tippers, pick-ups and enclosed panel vans (with twin sliding load doors) were all available on the same tiny six foot wheelbase; even a tall Luton body was possible on this minuscule chassis. In July 1993, Rascal production was halted in Luton to make room for extra Frontera production, but the overseas models carried on in Japan until 1999. Despite the miniature size, incredibly, the internal van capacity was 93ft³.

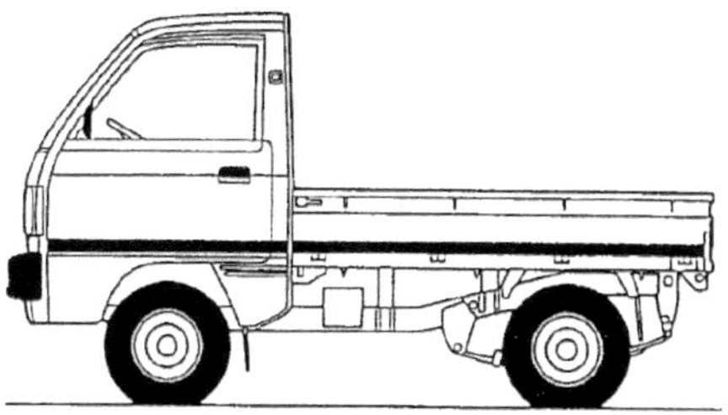

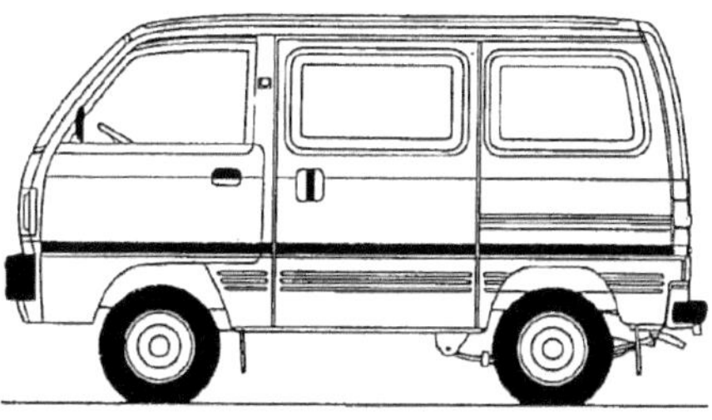

The tiny Rascal was available as a pick-up and enclosed van.

Danbury Conversions produced an extended pop-up roof to the van body and fitted it out to form a small camper with side glazing and curtains. Remarkably, Romahome produced a demountable Bambi camper-van for the rear buck on the pick-up version, complete with cooker, toilet and beds. The spare wheel was often mounted on the front panel, and an awning was possible for much needed extra room. Eldiss produced an even bigger body for the Rascal. This and the Romahome both had a section of the fibre-glass accommodation extending up and over the cab – a real worry on a windy motorway, flat out approaching 60mph ...

A Rascal enclosed panel van on lightweight flower delivery duties in Glasgow, Scotland. Note Vauxhall badge is now a transfer below the grille, plus a Griffin transfer above the grille.

RASCAL BODY TYPES: van, tipper/pick-up, Luton, camper-vans: 1986-1993; **manufactured at**: Luton by Bedford then IBC; **number produced**: worldwide numbers not known.
PERFORMANCE: **top speed**: 70mph (114kph); **average economy**: 30-45mpg.
PRICE AT LAUNCH: £3650 + VAT (van), £3315 + VAT (pick-up).
MEASUREMENTS: **length**: 3.29/3.25m (van/pick-up); **width**: 4ft 7in/1.4m (strictly two-seater up front!); **height**: 1.78m (panel van); **wheelbase**: 6ft½in (1.84m) (both); **weight**: 1675-1730lb (760/785kg) (pick-up/van); **wheels**: 12in; **turning circle**: 30.2ft (9.2m); **fuel capacity**: 8.1 gallons (36.5 litres); **internal capacity**: 93ft^3.
TECHNICAL: **engine types**: 970cc, four-cyl, petrol; **gearbox**: five-speed manual, four-speed manual optional; **suspension**: independent MacPherson struts with coil (front), semi-elliptic four-leaf (rear); **brakes**: front disc, rear drum.
TRIM: cloth, vinyl (no cost option).
KEY OPTIONAL EXTRAS: four-speed manual (no cost), ladder rack, internal van racking kits, heavy-duty battery, vinyl seats (no cost), tailgate wash/wipe with heated rear window (van), tonneau cover (pick-up), lamp guards, five-speed overdrive (£60).

Media advertising slogans (all van types)

Petrol or diesel, your best buy is Bedford (CA)
The luxury caravan with built in independence (CA Dormobile)
For happy-go-lucky holidays pile into a Bedford 12-seater (CA)
We're away exploring in our Dormobile (CA)
Sun, fun and a genuine Dormobile (CA)
Bedford, easy as a car to drive (CA)
Presenting Europe's great new force: The Bedford CF Brigade (CF)
Cost less, carry more, run on low cost petrol (CA Mk3)
Unbeatable value for money! (CF Special)
Five star luxury on wheels (CF motor caravan)
More style. More comfort. And truck engineering (KB)
Carrying 7 people in luxury needn't be a stretch (Albany)
Now appearing all over town, due to popular demand (Midi)
The 24-hour day Midi. It just goes on and on (Midi)
Get your business into better shape (Midi)
The Rascal. A real half-tonner (Rascal)

The mid-1980s Bedford van range just before the demise of the CF. The HA and Chevanne had by now been deleted.

Bibliography

Vauxhall 1857-1946, LC Darbyshire, Vauxhall Motors, 1946
The Vauxhall Companion, Kenneth Ullyett, Stanley Paul, 1971
Vauxhall, The Postwar Years, Trevor Alder, Haynes Publishing, 1991
The Vauxhall, Peter Hull, Shire Publications, 1992
Vauxhall, Stuart Fergus Broatch, Sutton Publishing, 1997
The Vauxhall File, Eric Dymock, Dove Publishing, 1999
Vauxhall Cars, 1945-1964, Earnshaw & Berry, Trans Pennine Publishing, 2000
Vauxhall Cars, 1965-1984, Alan Earnshaw & Robert W Berry, Nostalgia Road, 2013
Vauxhall, model by model from 1903, Eric Dymock, Dove Publishing, 2016
Vauxhall Cars, James Taylor, Shire Publications, 2021
Car magazine
Popular Motoring magazine
Practical Motorist magazine
Motor magazine
Autocar magazine
Autocar & Motor magazine
What Car? magazine

Plus hundreds of Vauxhall factory brochures, various Transport Source Book reprint collections, imcdb.org website, howmanyleft.com website, and not forgetting the superb Vauxpedianet.uk website

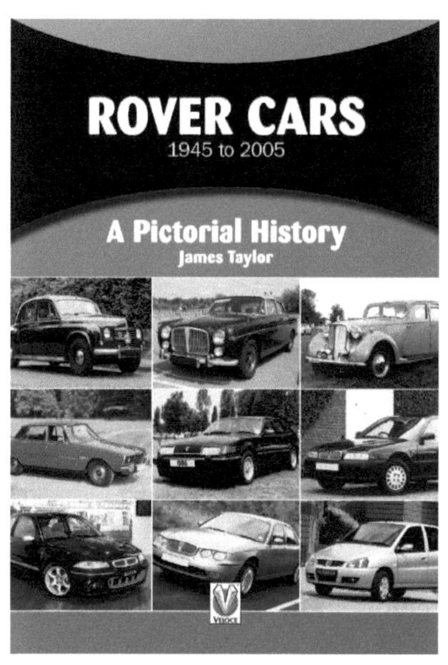

ISBN: 978-1-787116-09-2
Paperback • 21x14.8cm • 80 pages
• 300 pictures

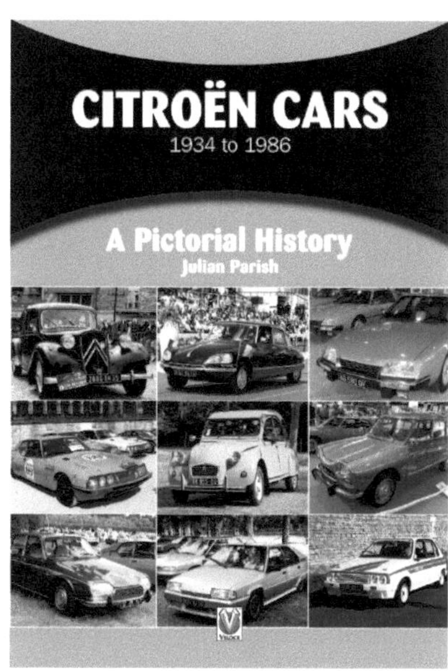

ISBN: 978-1-787116-36-8
Paperback • 21x14.8cm • 152 pages
• 350 pictures

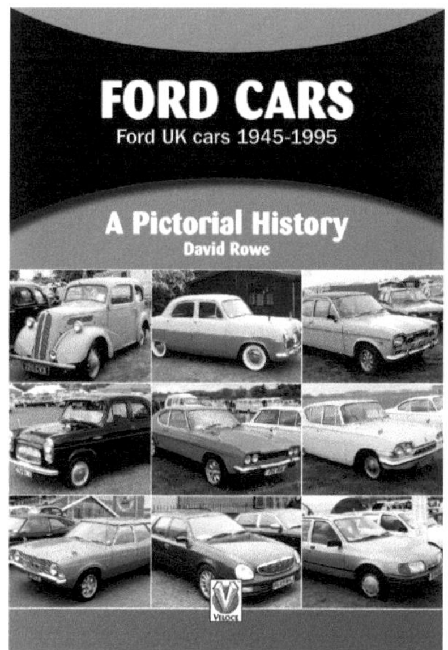

ISBN: 978-1-787116-42-9
Paperback • 21x14.8cm • 160 pages
• 330 pictures

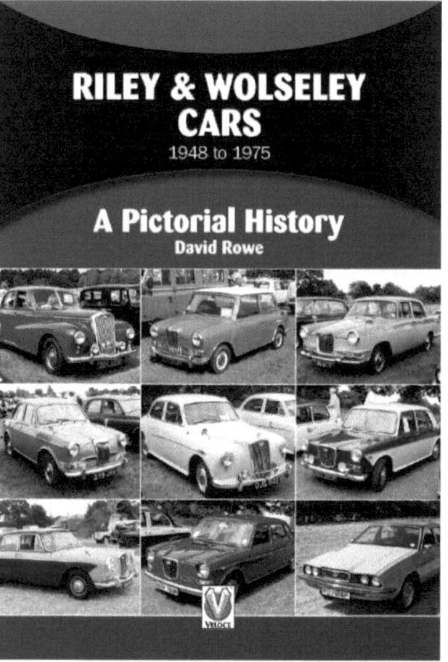

ISBN: 978 1 787117 91-4
Paperback • 21x14.8cm • 104 pages
• 352 colour and b&w pictures

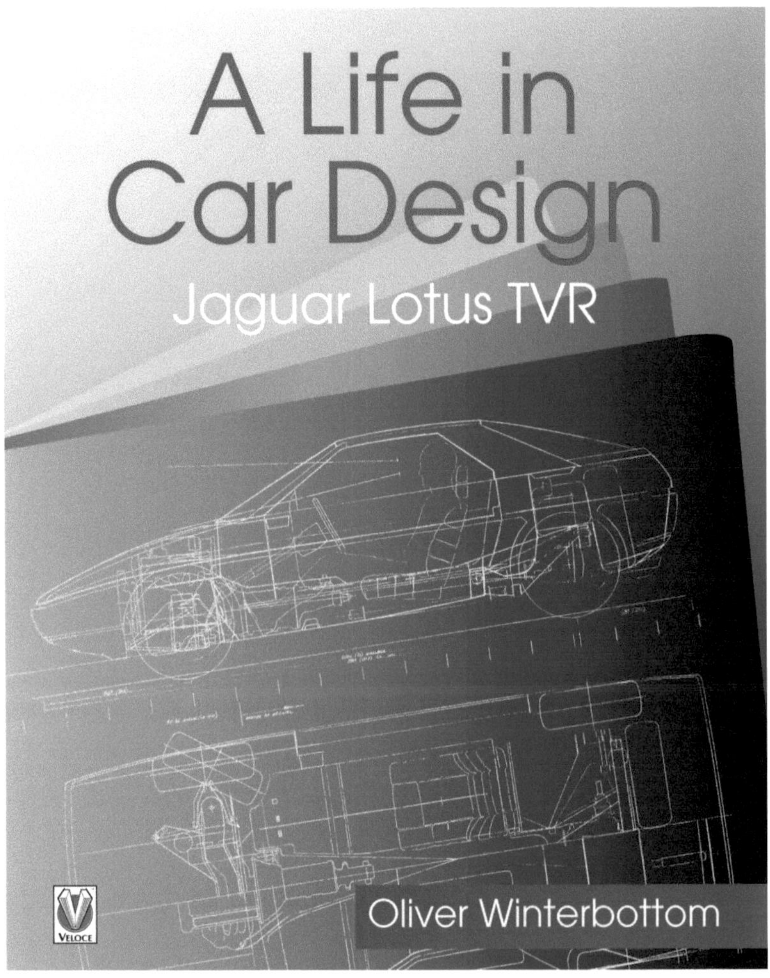
A Life in
Car Design
Jaguar Lotus TVR
Oliver Winterbottom
VELOCE

Index